CHARLES PERCY OF ILLINOIS

1970

CHARLES PERCY
OF ILLINOIS

by David Murray

HARPER & ROW, PUBLISHERS

NEW YORK, EVANSTON, AND LONDON

FIRST EDITION

LIBRARY OF CONGRESS CATALOG CARD NUMBER: 68-15967

B-S

To Corallie

Contents

vii

Illustrations follow page 52

Acknowledgments

With any political biography, particularly one appearing in an election year, the words "authorized" and "unauthorized" are often flung about with abandon. They are, in my view, both pejorative. "Authorized" implies that the subject of the biography has been leaning over the writer's shoulder, or that the author has taken money from the subject or that the subject has required that his imprimatur be placed on the final version. Or all three.

At the same time, "unauthorized" carries with it the connotation of a "hatchet job" or of backstairs gossip.

This book is "unauthorized" only in the sense that at no time did Senator Percy or any member of his staff ask to pass on it, but it is "authorized" to the extent that Senator Percy knew of its preparation and helped with interviews as often as his crowded schedule would permit. He further instructed members of his staff to provide me with assistance in gathering research materials within the limits of the time they could take from their regular duties in his Washington and Chicago offices. My special thanks for this cooperation go to Tom Houser, Calvin Fentress, Scott Cohen and Claudia Bourne for their assistance, as well as to all the others who answered a lot of damn-fool questions.

I am also grateful to members of the Percy family who permitted interviews, particularly Mrs. Elizabeth Percy, Sharon Percy Rockefeller, David and Carol Guyer and John Guyer, all of whom spoke frankly and readily about the ways in which Charles Percy had entered their lives.

My colleagues of the press were also helpful, especially David S. Broder of the Washington *Post* and Stephen Hess of Harvard University, who took time to give aid and comfort despite the fact that they were up to their antlers in publishing their own book, *The Republican Establishment.*

Thanks also must go to James F. Hoge, Jr., managing editor, and Kenneth Towers, city editor, of the Chicago *Sun-Times,* who juggled editorial schedules to clear time for writing and research and provided many valuable suggestions. Help also came from Basil Talbott, Jr. and Morton Kondracke. And a special debt of gratitude is owed John Dreiske, *Sun-Times* political editor, who gave a refugee from the 1966 New York newspaper holocaust unstintingly of the knowledge and wisdom that come from thirty years of covering Illinois and national politics.

Some of the above have read portions of this book prior to publication, but any errors are of course my sole responsibility.

Evan Thomas, my editor at Harper & Row, was patient and astute in providing encouragement, suggestions and ideas.

My gratitude also goes to Mrs. Lucille Krieske, who typed the final manuscript with accuracy, efficiency and dispatch, no small task in the last rush to meet deadlines.

Finally, a word of thanks to Jane, Davy and Catharine Murray, who kept interruptions at a minimum while their father was working, and to Corallie Hanly Murray, who good-humoredly put up with what my agent, Sterling Lord, accurately calls "the terrible emotional commitment" involved in writing a book.

D.M.

Wilmette, Illinois
December, 1967

CHARLES PERCY OF ILLINOIS

CHAPTER *1*

Washington Express

There were still ten days to go until the election, and the shining campaign train was bucketing across the Illinois prairie, fat and sassy and warm under the Indian summer sun. Inside the train there was, among the campaign staff, a political Indian summer, but it was just as fat, sassy and warm as the fields and pastures and little towns alongside the tracks.

The polls showed the candidate with a comfortable lead. The campaign itself had faltered shortly before, as the head of the ticket emerged from personal despair, but now it had gathered momentum, and in this three-ring, windup, zigzag, ding-dong tour around the state, the campaign workers basked in the crowds who came to see and to listen, ever growing in numbers, ever growing in enthusiasm.

On the first afternoon, the shadows at the edges of the cornfields began to stretch out as the sun dropped in the sky and the riders in the club car—mostly campaign aides and reporters—were beginning to relax, to order drinks in paper cups and to talk a little politics. The train was moving along at a good clip, but not as fast as the talk, which leapfrogged beyond the whistle-stop prairie towns with names like Minonk and Belleville and Mattoon and Carbondale and Alton. In these penultimate hours of the long campaign, thoughts and words were moving in time and space beyond Election Day, beyond Illinois, beyond even the United States Senate itself.

1

Now, with only the most incredible kind of miscalculation or disaster apparently standing between the candidate and victory, the talk turned to 1968, to 1972, to the chances that Illinois Republicans might, for the first time since Ulysses S. Grant, win the Presidency itself.

Near the bar in the club car stood a knot of newspapermen, some drawn from other major cities, others Chicago reporters who had covered this race from its outset. One of the Easterners proffered the thought that, with the GOP in such dismal national shape, it was "hard not to go along with some of these bright young moderates."

A Chicago writer admitted this might be true, but he added that he was not convinced of the virtues of the particular candidate on this particular campaign train.

"Well," replied the Easterner, "the vessels of salvation aren't always what we might choose."

Whatever the size, depth and configuration of Charles Harting Percy as a vessel of salvation for the Republican party nationally, it was more than apparent that in this year of grace 1966 he was being looked at as a length of political timber which might, if he won and if he could take it, be felled, sawed, turned and carved into an important component of the bandwagon which GOP moderates across the nation hoped to ride to victory in 1968. And on that October afternoon the job that most of those present were talking about was the Presidential nomination itself.

At first look, Percy seemed, paradoxically, both an odd and obvious choice as a Presidential tree. He was still untried—not only in the Senate but in any other public office. His campaign speeches were often monuments to vapidity, designed to woo and persuade in ringing tones, but seldom to startle and never to offend. And yet he was already a national figure, a businessman who appeared on the "Ten Top . . ." lists of countless Jaycee organizations, of groups like the Rotarians or the Kiwanis or the Lions. And two years before, with the albatross of Barry Goldwater hanging around his neck, he had gone down swinging in the race for Governor of Illinois. The business world and the politicians knew him as the man who had, with only a small amount of help, convinced the highly sensitive American photographic industry that it would thrive, rather than starve, if tariff laws were eased and German and Japanese competition encouraged.

In this 1966 race for the Senate seat held by the venerable, literate and professional Paul H. Douglas, Percy, for good or ill, was what Jimmy Breslin of the New York *World Journal Tribune* called "the candidate of all the nice white people." Although he had not himself openly courted the white backlash vote, he had equivocated on the immensely thorny issue of open occupancy. But at the same time he had made inroads into the slavishly Democratic Negro wards on Chicago's South and West Sides, still seething from the summer's rioting and the violence that had accompanied the open-housing marches into the lily-white suburban neighborhoods.

On foreign policy he spoke with the authority of a man who had built a large overseas business as president of Bell & Howell and who, on numerous trips abroad, had spoken with statesmen in most parts of the world. He espoused issues which to traditional Republicans were anathema—eventual Communist Chinese membership in the United Nations, increased East-West trade, escalation of peace efforts in Vietnam through something called an "all-Asian peace conference." This proposal had the endorsement of Asian statesmen, former President Dwight D. Eisenhower, the GOP House-Senate Conference and even—although grudgingly—President Lyndon B. Johnson. But while he spoke in dovelike tones, on this downstate trip, he was also to appeal to a still-strong streak of Midwest isolationism by wondering aloud why it was the United States continued to trade with countries which traded with North Vietnam.

To much of the nation, then, and to many Illinois voters, he was the very model of modern young Republicanism—moderate, articulate, still youthful (just forty-seven), his political letter sweater emblazoned with a big "E" for Eisenhower.

To others, he was shallow, a vacillator who shifted and hedged his position with the political winds on such issues as reapportionment, open housing and conservation of the Indiana Dunes, that great stretch of recreation land at the south end of Lake Michigan, which Douglas was fighting an often lonely battle to keep out of the hands of the private and industrial developers and to turn into a national park. (Percy had angered Illinois conservation-minded voters— many Republicans among them—when he said during the campaign that Douglas should be retired because he was "lost in the sand dunes of Indiana.")

"A cleaned-up Dick Nixon," one Chicago editor called him during the campaign. And on this campaign trip, Jimmy Breslin was to make readers of the Chicago *Sun-Times* and other newspapers chuckle (or turn purple) when he wrote that Percy's style "is to be white, look nice, say nothing and win."

What had brought Chuck Percy to this point in history, where victory was within his grasp for a Senate seat, to a point where he would parry, but with eyes shining, all questions about the Presidency in 1968 or 1972? The transubstantiation from camera maker to candidate had not been instantaneous, but other businessmen had, with varying degrees of success, entered politics and failed to come as far as Percy had come on this October day.

It had been a long and sometimes lonely trip. In the mare's-nest that is Illinois Republican politics, Percy, when he made the decision to go after the Governor's chair, had few friends and fewer firm political allies. Yet a combination of changing tides, conservatism bordering on reaction among GOP professionals, hard work and a large handout from Lady Luck won him the nomination. To become the Republican candidate, it was expedient for him to sit on the fence while the national battle raged over the issue of Goldwater. He pledged to abide by the choice of the convention at San Francisco, and that was the Senator from Arizona, a man whose ideas and philosophies generally were as different from Percy's as Senator Henry Cabot Lodge's were from President Wilson's.

The pledge made him enemies among the national Republicans who should have been his friends—Governor William Scranton of Pennsylvania, Governor Nelson Rockefeller of New York, Senator Jacob Javits of New York—but it also put him in a position where the conservatives of the party could not revile him, as they did Rockefeller and Governor George Romney of Michigan, for refusing to support Goldwater. But Percy was not so much identified with Goldwater that he would be unacceptable to the party's liberal and moderate wings, those who were anxious to exorcise the ghost of political polarization that had lost the Republicans the 1964 election—not only the Presidency but right across the board, from the Senate and the House of Representatives down to more than six hundred seats in state legislatures throughout the country.

Percy's decision to make the race for the U.S. Senate had, it is probably reasonable to assume, cost him the life of his daughter. While the crime on September 18, 1966, is still unsolved a year and a half later, it is hard to imagine that if Percy were not a public figure, Valerie Percy would have been murdered in her bed. The words "sympathy vote" do no honor to Valerie Percy, her father, the voters or the person who employs them. But the murder was a factor in bringing Percy to this point in his career.

It had become almost a cliché in Illinois to say that Percy, with his business success, his clean-cut good looks, his attractive family, and with all the trappings of success, was "too good to be true."

Most voters see in candidates the mirror, one way or another, of themselves, of their aspirations and frustrations, or their achievements and shortcomings. What a candidate is or how he looks or the way he talks is a reflection of what they themselves would like to be or fear they are. Eisenhower was a national hero, the chieftain with stars in his headdress, the Mittyesque incarnation of duty, honor, country. Harry S Truman, on the other hand, was the blunt-spoken, warts-and-all plain man, the merchant who fell on hard times, the usher at the church door on Sunday morning. John F. Kennedy was the embodiment of all that was best in the Depression-reared, war-tested generation; like, as the young voter thought, calling to like.

How to fit Chuck Percy into this mind's-eye picture of the Illinois voter in 1964 and 1966? His was a success story, from Depression poverty to millionaire at the age of forty, head of a photogenic and attractive family, a clean-limbed, deep-voiced, athletic extrovert.

This appealed to many voters, but to others, even many Republicans, particularly those in the comfortable North Shore Chicago suburbs, the remark at cocktail parties and dinner parties echoed and re-echoed for three years: "There's *something* about Chuck Percy!" This "something"—which of course did not extend to all Republicans or all Illinoisans—was what often seemed to be a non-human side to Percy, as if, in the words of one Chicago political writer, "a big public-relations computer had produced a humanoid candidate."

It was a factor up until the morning of September 18, 1966, when, suddenly, over the Sunday-morning coffee cups, the word came of Valerie Percy's murder. For the terrible three days that followed, all anyone had to do was to open a newspaper or turn on a television set to be able to feel an empathy with Chuck Percy and his family, to be able to look on him not as those who "went without the meat, and cursed the bread" looked on Edwin Arlington Robinson's Richard Cory, but rather to say, "There, but for the grace of God, go I."

What was more important in those three days was the deportment of Percy and his family. Like Mrs. John Kennedy and other members of the family at the time of the assassination, the Percys, particularly the candidate himself, seemed to find an almost frightening strength within themselves to carry on, to do what was expected of them in the all-searching publicity that accompanied every move. This, probably more than anything else, turned half-envy into admiration and eliminated, in many minds, the "something" that had rankled about Percy.

It had been three years since Percy had begun what in effect was one campaign to seek office. Now, in September, under a cloud of personal tragedy, and in October, as the race pounded down the home stretch, there was being revealed for the first time a man with a spark, with a visceral ambition and motivation, a man who was quite patently not just another political candidate, but someone who, for better or worse, was a man to be reckoned with.

How far his spark could carry him was still not known. But there was no longer any doubt that the spark was there.

CHAPTER 2

The Human Tragedy

In a steel cabinet in the office of the Coroner, County of Cook, State of Illinois, there is a file labeled "PERCY, Valerie Jeanne." Among the other papers in it is one—a single sheet—on which three paragraphs appear, and the last sentence of the second paragraph reads:

"This occurrence took place on Sept. 18, A.D. 1966, at or about 5:15 o'clock A.M."

The fifteen spare, cold words of forensic prose—the verdict of the coroner's jury—are the vertebrate structure of a major crime, a family's ordeal, a political bench mark. Whether it is measured in political terms or in human terms, whether it is remembered in terms of a brutal crime or in terms of a vanished life that had just been beginning to fulfill itself, the murder of Valerie Percy is a caesura; before it, in the lives of Charles Percy, of his wife and children, of the dozens and scores and hundreds of lives that had touched Valerie's life, there was one thing; after it, there was another, and the two will never be joined.

A year and a half later, it is impossible to say exactly how great an influence the fact of the murder and those ghastly days that followed it had on Percy as a candidate, as a Senator and as a human being. But a year and half later, there is every evidence that it played a major role not only in the campaign but in subsequent events and attitudes as well. A Chicagoan who travels about the country finds, for one thing, that when Percy's name comes up in

7

conversation, others want to know how much progress has been made toward a solution. In 1967 Loraine Percy disliked intensely any discussion of Presidential politics involving her husband, and the private explanation was that the combination of the memory of Valerie and the memory of President Kennedy's assassination filled her with overwhelming concern for security. In the opinion of many who followed Percy's career before and after Valerie's murder, it is a central fact of life, a human and emotional and political sea change that cannot be ignored. Tragedy, according to Aristotle, evokes pity or fear and acts as a catharsis to the emotions. But tragedy is also drama, and the human tragedy that was acted out at Percy's Kenilworth home in those fall days left an indelible imprint on the memories of all concerned.

Time has a way of building up emotional muscle to wrestle with separation and grief, to replace bitterness and emptiness with pleasant, nostalgic memories. But memory is the key. A reporter, for example, remembers Valerie listening as the reporter and one of her father's campaign aides exchanged mock-insulting banter about a speech the candidate had just finished delivering one summer day before the Chicago Rotary Club. Valerie listened, a little unsure of how she should react, and then giggled when she decided, apparently, that it was just another part of the new life, the political life, that she was beginning to find frustrating at times but fascinating and always fun.

The same reporter remembers campaigning with her and her father for a day and then coming home at night and remarking to his wife over a predinner drink that if their own daughters grew up like Valerie, he would be a happy man indeed.

These are one man's memories, and others have their own, particularly Percy himself, who, in conversation or in thought, brings them forth as old Nantucket whaling men used to hold pieces of scrimshaw in their hands, caressing them to conjure up a thousand sights and sounds and smells of the venturesome, youthful seas.

To Percy, Valerie and Sharon particularly were links to a younger, less structured life, a time of bright challenge, a time for Dantès to cry out in the grotto of Monte Cristo that the world was his. In them he saw reflected that younger time, just as others could look at Sharon and see Valerie looking at them out of her twin sister's eyes.

But the caesura is there.

It was a quiet, fairly typical dinner party, that night of September 17. It was certainly repeated, that Saturday night, in several dozen homes on the North Shore, in several hundred in the Chicago area, in several thousand across the country.

Loraine Percy acted as hostess for Valerie, who was entertaining two young men—campaign workers and good friends. The talk was typical, too, although of necessity heavily tinged with politics and the campaign. They talked of Sharon's summer in Africa, of friends, of the shoes and ships and sealing wax in all their lives that make for conversation. There was laughter at the private jokes that young people who are close friends always seem to collect, and at the end of it the two guests drove off into the soft, early fall night. Sharon, who had been out with friends, returned early.

Loraine, Sharon and Valerie talked among themselves for a bit, then Sharon and Valerie went upstairs to their rooms to get ready for bed.

As Sharon was preparing for bed, she remembered that she had borrowed a raincoat from Valerie and picked it up and walked down the hall to Valerie's room; she knocked and walked in and tossed the coat onto Valerie's bed.

"Don't put it on the bed," Valerie told her. "It'll get wrinkled."

So Sharon hung the coat up in a closet and walked back down the hall to her own room.

Percy, who had been making a series of campaign appearances in Chicago during the day, returned shortly after midnight. He gave a cursory check to the grounds as he walked from the gravel driveway to the west door of the house, which gives onto a narrow hallway. The check was more for domestic reasons than for security; for one thing, Mark as often as not left his bicycle out and it had to be put away.

Inside, Loraine was waiting up for him and together they watched about an hour of *Sun-Times* columnist Irv Kupcinet's television interview show, a popular late-Saturday-night pastime in the Chicago area. Then they, too, went up the stairs, turned down the hall away from the children's rooms and went to bed in their own room.

From that point, about 1:30 A.M., until "at or about 5:15 o'clock A.M.," only one person alive knows precisely what happened.

Percy is a heavy sleeper, while his wife is a light one. So, when there came from down the hall what Mrs. Percy later described as "a low moan," it was she who awakened. But the moan was not loud enough to penetrate through her drowsiness to the built-in alarm signals in every mother's mind. Another moan a little later did penetrate, however, and she was able to identify it as coming from Valerie's room. She got out of bed and walked down the hall, calling softly as she went, "Valerie! Val!"

As she walked into Valerie's room, she was grabbed by shock and fright. Beside Valerie's bed stood a man, wearing a short, light-colored shirt or jacket, checked or patterned in a darker color, and dark slacks. The only other thing she could see was that the shirt or jacket was short-sleeved.

The intruder must have heard her gasp or move or breathe, because he whirled around and the beam from his flashlight caught her full in the eyes. It had the effect of a jack light on a deer in the night forest. Mrs. Percy stood, by her own account, "frozen for a moment," which was all that the intruder needed to push by her and run out the door and down the stairs. When the light was gone, Mrs. Percy recovered enough to call to Percy, who remembers being jolted awake by "a scream of terror and by the wail of the siren." Mrs. Percy left Valerie's room and tripped an alarm in the hall, which set off a siren mounted on top of the house. The system is not uncommon in the small North Shore suburban towns, where police patrols at night are spotty at best.

Percy leaped out of bed and ran down the hall to Valerie's room. He looked quickly around the room, briefly examined Valerie's still form, then ran back down the hall to the telephone by his bedside. He jerked the receiver off the phone and pressed the "Operator" button at the bottom of the touch-tone panel. When he got the Kenilworth police station, he gave a brief account of what had happened and then hung up. He called a doctor who lived nearby and a Christian Science practitioner.

His first instinct, he recalled later, was to pursue the killer, to try and head him off before he left the grounds of "Windward." So he left Mrs. Percy with Valerie and ran down the stairs and into the hall, where he saw the west door, the one he had locked less than five hours earlier, still locked. He called to Henry Witting, the Percys' English houseman, whose living quarters were over the garage, just a few feet above Percy's head. But another door, at the southeast corner of the house, was wide open.

It had been Percy's intention to chase the intruder, but now, as he stood in the open door, looking out into the night and listening to the wind off the lake sighing in the tops of the elm trees overhead, he was gripped with a sudden thought: Suppose the killer were still in the house? He could see nothing and hear nothing to indicate the intruder was outside in the dark, and he also recalled another horrible crime which had rocked Chicago and the country just two months earlier. This was the murder of eight student nurses from the South Side Community Hospital. They were strangled and stabbed to death in a long night of murder. The crime, as it was for millions of other Chicagoans, was still fresh in Percy's mind.

"I thought of the dozen different directions the killer could have gone in his escape," Percy said later, "and the hundred places he could have been hiding. I thought of the murders of the nurses and thought that the killer could still be in the house."

So he turned back from the open door and crossed the living room and mounted the stairs again. His aim now was to gather the family together, so that if the killer still might be in the house, he could not attack other members of the family one by one. Roger was at college in Menlo Park, California, and Mark was on what is known as an "overnight" at a neighbor's house. Percy called to Mrs. Percy, Sharon and Gail and got them together in the Percys' bedroom. A minute later, they were joined by Witting, and when the houseman had arrived to provide extra male protection for the women, Percy again left the room to make a search of the house. He found nothing, no trace of the person, presumably a man, who had entered in what was, in more ways than one, the darkest hour, had beaten Valerie on the head with a heavy instrument and then had stabbed her fourteen times in the chest and abdomen and left her dying in her bed.

All this had taken only a few minutes—no one can say with complete certainty just how long. The police records at the Kenilworth station show the call was received at 5:15 A.M. Patrolman Gary Wolff was the first officer to arrive on the scene, just as Percy was concluding his search of the house. Wolff was taken upstairs to Valerie's room. He bent over the girl and made a quick examination. He thought, he said later, he had detected "a faint pulse," and immediately called for a doctor and ambulance as well as for more help. But it had been too late from the outset. Valerie, mercifully, had been all but unconscious from the time the killer had struck her on the head the first time, and no doctor, then or later, could have saved her.

Somehow, like ghosts, like automatons, the family managed to get through the next few hours. There were people to be called—family members and people like Sharon's still unofficial fiancé, John D. Rockefeller IV, running his campaign for the West Virginia Legislature. He was one of the first to be called, and he, too, proved to be a source of strength.

There was his wife's family, the Guyers—Carol and David in New York and John and Diane in California—and Percy's own kin, Howard and Elaine Percy from St. Louis and Doris Percy Strauss and her husband Robert from Wisconsin. And then there were the political allies and the old friends and associates from Bell & Howell.

Paul Douglas was campaigning in East St. Louis, Illinois, a Negro Democratic stronghold. When he heard the news, he immediately sent a telegram to Kenilworth: "My heart goes out to you over your cruel and terrible loss. My deep sympathy and condolences to you both. I am calling off all my campaigning. May God bless you and keep you both."

These were the first; later there would be more, but these were the first.

But it was not only a death in the family. This was murder, too, and the state began to move in as soon as the reports were made and as soon as the various branches of the various law-enforcement agencies could begin. In her room, the body of Valerie Jeanne Percy became the property of the state, to be photographed, fingerprinted, examined. Cook County Coroner Dr. Andrew J. Toman announced to the waiting reporters at midmorning that Valerie's assailant had struck her twice on the head with the classic "blunt instrument" and had also stabbed her fourteen times in the chest and abdomen. Robbery, he said, was apparently not a motive since no jewelry was disturbed and Valerie's wallet, with money still in it, was apparently untouched.

Chief Robert H. Daley of the Kenilworth Police Department, who later became Village Manager, said the intruder "obviously came into the house to murder someone," but he could not say who—then or later.

The statement was typical of the rash of observations, remarks and rumors that saturated the newspapers and the airwaves and the rumor factories in Chicago during the next few days. There was surmise and there were false clues—a pocket knife, a broken scissors blade, a moccasin, footprints. These were supposed to be physical clues of great importance. There were also supposed to have been eyewitness reports, "mystery witnesses," such as a man to whom Valerie spoke on the elevated train coming home late a few evenings earlier.

But when it was over, when the lie-detector tests had been given to campaign aides who had known Valerie well, when the "physical clues" had been checked out and examined, only one sure, certain piece of knowledge remained: that Valerie Jeanne Percy had been bludgeoned and stabbed by someone who broke into the house by cutting a screen door and a glass panel in a terrace door. There was nothing beyond that—all the physical clues led nowhere.

Several weeks later, Richard Ogilvie, the Sheriff of Cook County who was campaigning for the job of County Board President, was asked by a reporter what kind of progress he felt was being made in the investigation. "We're going to have to get awfully lucky in this one," Ogilvie said. It was a good summation of what law-enforcement officials had felt practically since the first few hours. The investigation was to continue, as much as it could continue, for months afterward, with a special office set up in Kenilworth just to look into new reports, new breaks, new results of interrogations of suspects from different parts of the country who might have been picked up on other crimes and who might have admitted being in or near the Chicago area on the night of September 18.

It was about all that could be done. Percy himself said later that they did not know who had been the intended victim—it might have been any other member of the family, or might have been someone bent on killing or hurting anyone close to a successful businessman and popular public figure. All that could be expected, if that was the correct expression, was that somewhere, sometime again, the assailant who had struck once would strike again in a similar manner, would be caught and would, under questioning, provide corroborative evidence that he was a logical suspect in the murder of Valerie Percy.

Even from the beginning, there were no "good" suspects, no "solid" clues. Not that the case wasn't pushed as hard as it could have been. The present-day Chicago Police Department did not achieve its deserved reputation for dedication and efficiency through clever public-relations men. And the department's crime laboratory is one of the best arms of that excellent force.

But it was a very bad case.

Inside the house, the family sat, greeting their guests with an embrace, listening to the words which, as always, were totally inadequate. The messages arrived from Senator Everett McKinley Dirksen, from Governor Otto Kerner, the Democrat who had defeated Percy two years before, from Mayor Richard J. Daley, from former Vice President Richard M. Nixon, from Jacqueline and Robert Kennedy, and a host of others.

Members of the Percy campaign staff came to offer their own comfort, and also to help out in whatever way they could. Campaign manager Thomas Houser, Calvin Fentress, Scott Cohen and Patricia Oakley, Percy's secretary, came, not so much as political associates but as friends of the dead girl. Cohen, close to tears, was asked by reporters whether the murder meant an end to campaigning.

"He's still in the running for United States Senator," he answered. "But we haven't been talking campaign plans in there today." It would be a good ten days before the campaign was discussed again.

But other plans were made. Late in the afternoon, Cohen announced that there would be a four-hour "visitation" at a Wilmette funeral home two miles away on Monday evening and that a private family memorial service would be held at the Kenilworth Union church, three blocks from "Windward."

It is a nondenominational church, and since the Christian Science faith has no funeral service in its liturgy, the Union church was picked both because it would provide sufficient space for those who were expected to attend Valerie's memorial rites and because a service of prayer, music and Bible readings would be most suitable in a church which was not governed by the liturgy of a particular faith.

Inside the house, the family sat, shrunken in aspect, drawn into themselves, with shock serving as a kind of armor plate for emotion. Now and again, Percy would read from the Bible, but for the most part it was a time of automatic response to friends and family, a time for cups of coffee to be placed in front of them and then, as often as not, forgotten, a time when food was nibbled at but not really eaten.

By Monday morning the shock had worn off and the Percys were pushing back into the real world. Neighbors came to call, bringing with them tangible expressions of human sympathy—a ham, a jar of homemade soup, cakes, cookies. Some freedom of movement had started inside the house, and there was none of Sunday's sullen, semicomatose apathy.

Seldom were there more than a dozen people in the large, bright living room, with its plate-glass windows looking out on the sweep of Lake Michigan, whitecapped in the stiff breeze, or in the paneled, book-lined library, where the family had spent much of Sunday. Those who had come talked in low voices, and, except for occasional brief visits by detectives, it was a personal time.

Two schoolmates of Mark's rode their bicycles up to the rope strung across the driveway to keep the newsmen at a distance. They had come at the request of his home-room teacher at Joseph Sears School in Kenilworth, they said, to bring his books so that he wouldn't get behind in his studies. A grocery order arrived, and it was noted that it contained several two-pound cans of coffee. Loraine Percy a few weeks before had complained that one of the troubles with campaigning was the amount of coffee she had to drink with women's groups—"sometimes thirty cups a day." But that was for votes; this was for survival and to keep the hands busy so that the mind would not think too much.

Then, suddenly, it was time to face the world again, to stand up in public at a funeral home and greet people, not the close friends who had come to the house, but the business and political friends, the acquaintances whose more distant relationship with the family and with Valerie had not let them come to "Windward" to the more intimate surroundings of the Percy home. So for four hours, in a self-imposed ordeal that saw only an occasional break, Charles Percy stood at the head of a reception line, his eyes red-rimmed, his face grim, almost a death mask in comparison to the lively features of the campaigning politician he had been up until forty-eight hours before.

One by one, the visitors came through the line, murmuring the rote expressions that serve as passwords at rites of passage such as these. And, one by one, he answered them, saying things like:

"There has to be a reason for everything."

"We've been worried mostly about the children, how they would take it."

"We all have problems and we overcome them."

"The family has been wonderful."

It is perhaps cruel to set down these words so long after the fact, since they sound as banal as the phrases the visitors used. But in that atmosphere charged with emotion the wonder was that he could say anything at all, let alone give, as he did, a little comfort to those who had come to grieve with him. In Percy's time of personal trial, it was almost as if a curtain had been lifted and, for the first time, the man within had let himself be seen, and what was on display was something totally new.

Here was no longer a candidate whose bland phrases often sounded glib; here was no longer the candidate whom Paul Douglas later in the campaign equipped with a "Sunday-afternoon smile"; here was not the self-made millionaire with the well-trained voice and the well-trained hair. Here was a man with an inner fiber and strength that had not been on view before; hitherto it had been used often to satisfy a personal ambition that was not particularly reprehensible, but rather was the outward and visible sign of an inner-directed drive toward *something*, toward some vague, unknown goal which he liked to call "public service" and which others said was the Governor's chair or the U.S. Senate or the Presidency itself.

Long after the event, Percy's campaign manager, Thomas J. Houser, admitted in a conversation that he had not in five years of close association with Percy been able to figure out what the element was that drove Percy, what the fire was that gnawed at his vitals, that pushed him and led him toward a destiny which he could not himself see.

In *The Making of the President 1964*, Theodore H. White describes his own view of the image of politics. It is, he says, "an immense journey—the panorama of an endless wagon train, an enormous trek, a multitudinous procession of people larger and more confused than any of the primitive folk migrations."

At its head, White says, are the leaders, who from the top of a rise can see the terrain that lies beyond and can tell whether or not to flog their followers through the dangerous country or to let them stop and rest, "because they are entering fair fields and good hunting lands."

Until Percy achieved the United States Senate, he was not one of the leaders himself, but he sought to be one; from the multitude involved in the trek, he had to push his way forward, saying "Excuse me" where he could and sometimes shouldering aside those who, for one reason or another, lacked his powers. But to start the thrust forward to the head of the line of march takes an initial strength, an initial ambition. For most people, being part of the pack is enough; for Percy—as for most other successful politicians —it was not; a magic ingredient was needed to initiate the action of the political detergent.

In Percy's case, the causes can only be guessed at, but the guesses can be informed. And a major factor was Percy's youth and family life.

CHAPTER *3*

The Depression Cloud

"When my dad was getting ready to retire, I was trying to think of a retirement present for him, and I was having a hard time doing it. Then I remembered how we had lost our car during the Depression years and how Dad was so tight on gas all the time. He used to drive into a filling station and buy a dollar's worth, more or less. I can't remember him ever getting more than about five gallons at a time. So, when he retired, I gave Mother and Dad a Standard Oil credit card, with the bills sent directly to me. They were so proud, especially Dad, at the thought of being able to drive into a station and say 'Fill 'er up.' Just before he passed away, he and Mother took a trip in their car to Florida. Dad died on Christmas Eve in 1962. He'd just finished opening the presents, sitting there in his chair."

Charles Percy told this story to a reporter while the two of them were sitting in the camper truck that was used as a mobile headquarters during the Senate campaign in 1966. It was an afternoon in July, and Percy had spoken at a "Frontier Days" celebration in Libertyville, home of the late Adlai Stevenson, and had shaken hands at an air show in another town in northern Illinois. The reporter's notes contain a parenthetical observation that Percy was "very affected" when he talked about his father.

And another interviewer had a similar experience. William Trombley, in a *Saturday Evening Post* profile in 1963, described an incident in which Percy, relating how Edward Percy had worked a seven-day, eighty-four-hour week for $35 as a night clerk in a hotel

18

on the North Side of Chicago, had wept at the recollection. "To see him coming home then . . . he was so depressed," Percy said, the tears rolling down his cheeks. "I'm sorry. I didn't realize the memory of my father in those years could still arouse that much emotion."

In recent years, when Percy talked about his parents, he often gave the credit to his mother for being the strong, central figure during the bad years, but it was his father who brought out in him the strongest emotional responses. He remembered the cookies his mother made which he sold door to door (after a relief truck had dropped off a hundred-pound bag of sugar in error), but it was the memory of his father which brought the harsh bite of tears.

The relative poverty of the Percy family in the Depression was well known in Chicago before Percy entered public life, but the fact that the family once was on relief was not, for some reason. In 1964, during the gubernatorial campaign, one of his aides was amazed to hear that the candidate's family had received relief checks during the Depression. Why hadn't Percy mentioned it? "You didn't ask me," was Percy's reply, to which the aide retorted, with considerable accuracy: "You don't go around asking members of the Chicago Club if they've been on relief." But writer Hal Higdon noted in *The Reporter* in 1964 that after the aide had raised the point, Percy himself seldom missed a chance to raise it in speeches.

While Percy lived in Kenilworth, his mother was only a five-minute drive away, in a town house in Wilmette, the next village, a comfortable house which always seemed to have at least one grandchild dropping in to play or make lemonade or sit and chat. One day, in the summer of 1966, Mrs. Edward Percy sat in her living room and talked with a reporter, who wanted, among other things, to know about Percy's relationship with his father.

"He loved his father very much," she said. "He respected him. His father was strict and demanded obedience, but obedience brings respect and that brings forth love."

In an earlier conversation, Percy himself had said that his mother had held the family together during the Depression years.

"I wouldn't put it that way," Mrs. Percy said. "My husband did different things—selling paint and automobiles, working nights in a hotel. He did what he could. I don't believe we ever went to bed hungry. Oh, we didn't have as much to eat as we would have liked or often what we would have liked, and I did bake cookies for Chuck to sell. But we weren't any worse off than a lot of other people. We'd work and hope things would get better. We always felt there was a way out. We were optimistic."

She said that the lean years, when Percy's drive to excel in the marts of commerce became a necessity rather than an avocation, were good for her son. "Chuck always helped, and the Depression helped him; it spurred him on. He always made a lot of friends, and good reports about things he would do would come back to me. We had a family, and we were grateful that we could all stick together."

But the Depression had hit the Percy family at what, for Percy, the eldest child, must have been the worst possible age—twelve years. Percy was born in Pensacola, Florida, on September 27, 1919, and the family moved to Chicago, Elizabeth Percy's birthplace, when Chuck was an infant. Edward Percy became the cashier of a Chicago bank, and the family—a sister, Doris, born in 1920, and a brother, Howard, born a year later—lived in what could be described as comfortable circumstances. Elizabeth Percy was a violinist, and there were piano and clarinet lessons for young Charles (the nickname "Chuck" came later, with a business and political career). "We used to joke about the 'thousand-dollar piece'—a concerto that Charles learned to play. It was about the only classical piece he could play and a thousand dollars, we figured, was about what it had cost for him to learn it," Mrs. Percy said. It was a Rachmaninoff prelude, but his repertoire also included "Red Sails in the Sunset" and similar popular songs of the time.

In 1966 Percy took a reporter through some of the neighborhoods where he had lived as a boy. This was the Rogers Park section of Chicago, still within the city limits but where large apartment houses give way to semisuburban, tree-shaded streets with single-family and two-family houses. His running commentary was indicative of a childhood spent in middle-class surroundings—the school from which he had once been briefly suspended for an unremembered prank, the house where a friend lived who had a large collection of Tom Swift books, another house, larger than most, where a girl he knew lived (Percy remembered that the house seemed to him at the time to be the biggest he had ever seen).

Then came the Stock Market crash, and two years later, in 1931, the bank of which Edward Percy was an officer went under. In those days the woods were stiff with out-of-work cashiers from failed small banks, and the Percys' standard of living dropped rapidly. "I know what poverty can do to a family," Percy said once, talking of that time, "moving from one apartment or house to another, and every time the new one smaller and in a worse neighborhood than the one before. I know what it's like to have the phone cut off and the car repossessed because you can't pay the bills. I had a clarinet that was repossessed, too."

He remembered, too, a sameness in diet. To several interviewers, Percy recalled that Spanish rice was a staple and appeared so often on the dinner table that years later he could not bear to look a dish of it in the face. He also said once that Spanish rice was the cause of the only oath he ever remembered hearing his father utter. Once when Spanish rice showed up on the table for perhaps the sixth or seventh night in a row, Edward Percy started picking at his dinner before grace had been said. Elizabeth Percy asked if he couldn't "wait a moment and express your gratitude to God for what He's given us."

"I'll be damned," her husband said, "if I'm grateful for this."

Percy also said once that it was "the pleasure I found in meeting people, in talking to them," that had started him out in business for himself. At five years, he was selling *The Country Gentleman,* doing the lemonade-stand turn and various other selling jobs. He won a plaque from the publishers for selling the rurally oriented *Country Gentleman* to more city dwellers than any other urban-based sales-man in the country. On other, similar sales routes, his mother said, "he was always winning prizes—a watch, a bicycle, things like that."

He was a saver, too, Mrs. Percy said. "He wasn't stingy, but he saved his money. He was always ready for the big things because he saved on the little things." Once, when he was a teen-ager, his mother gave him a dime for bus fare because the weather was bitter cold that day, about fifteen degrees below zero, Mrs. Percy remembered. "I told him, 'You ride to school today,' but when he got home that night, he gave me the dime back. 'I'm no sissy!' he told me. He was shaking his fist at me, but he was laughing, too."

While he was a student at New Trier High School in Winnetka, Percy held as many as four jobs at the same time. Before he went to school, he stoked furnaces; at school, during free periods, he worked in the registrar's office; after school, he had a newspaper route; and evenings and weekends, he ushered at the movie theater in the Plaza del Lago, a small shopping center which lies between

Wilmette, where the family lived at the time, and Kenilworth, where he was to live when he had made his fortune.

Going back and forth to school, Percy saw every day a handsome stone house that stood beside Lake Michigan, and a Depression-born dream formed in his mind, the sort of dream every poor boy gets from time to time: "Someday, someday I'm going to . . ." One night at the theater, Percy saw the Kenilworth businessman who owned the house and said to him frankly, "Someday, I'm going to buy that house you live in." He did, too, after he became president of Bell & Howell. After Valerie's murder in 1966, he hung onto the house when other men would have sold it because of its associations. To those who asked whether he planned to sell it in the months that followed Valerie's death, Percy replied that there were no plans to sell it because the other children in the family looked on it as home and had too many happy associations with it. But other members of the family said it was Percy himself who, of all the family, was most determined to keep it. The house was sold, though, in the fall of 1967.

During the time when Charles Percy was working at multiple part-time jobs to help the family, Edward Percy was having his roughest time. In a nation with fifteen million unemployed in 1933, it was more than hard to sell paint to homeowners who were having trouble enough meeting the mortgage and rent bills. Selling autos to people who didn't know how long they might have their jobs was an equally difficult task. In those years, Edward Percy was not the only man in America who bought only a dollar's worth of gasoline at a time. So the onetime bank officer became a night clerk at a down-at-heels hotel on the North Side, a middle-aged man who could remember better times and better jobs, dragging himself home, bone-weary, every morning, with no time for his family. The current phrase for someone who gives up and lives on the dole is that he has "removed himself from the labor market." But Edward Percy, the proud Southerner whose father had served on the staff of General Robert E. Lee, stayed with his job, although it meant that he had little time for his wife and three children, a condition which bothered his elder son quite apparently more than he knew.

In writing about Charles Percy, there has always been the tendency to cast him in the mold of the Horatio Alger hero. *Time*, in a 1964 cover story, began its treatment with a long excerpt from

Ragged Dick; or Street Life in New York with the Bootblacks.
Even Loraine Percy said once that her husband's life "sounds like
a soap opera, doesn't it?" But there has to be more to it than that.

Dr. Robert Coles, the Harvard psychiatrist, has said that his dis-
cipline of medicine still does not know enough about the human mind
to be certain of what creates the drives that make a Claude Brown
or a Malcolm X emerge from the most desperate situations of
ghetto life to write *Manchild in the Promised Land* or become the
leader of Black Islam. Although the conditions are not completely
analogous, it would not be idle to try to seek the deep-buried motiva-
tions and traumas that moved a young, middle-class white American
as he moved through a comfortable childhood to a deprived adoles-
cence, burying himself in the work that once was fulfillment in itself
but which had become a necessity and a family responsibility at the
time when children are normally neither moved nor required to take
on heavy economic responsibilities. Couple this, too, with the daily
spectacle of a loved and respected father wearing himself out plod-
ding around the dull, quietly desperate water wheel that is always
unexpected in the Great American Dream.

Given an identical set of family and financial circumstances, had
Percy been born a half-dozen years earlier, it is fair to wonder
whether he might not well have become embittered and disillu-
sioned, possibly a campus Communist of the mid-thirties, crown-
ing his career with a semilethargic swimming about in a business
or academic backwater. Or, given the same background, but with a
birthday a half-dozen years later, might not his early drive to succeed
in selling have become diluted into an ambition to make money for
cars and dates, to move into a college world of fraternity parties and
an adult life of reasonable success in a well-established business?

In young Charles Percy's life there were some bench marks to
give a kind of dim insight—the only possible kind short of psycho-
analysis—into what gave him a driving ambition tempered with
a desire to help others, especially his family. On a number of occasions, for example, he told interviewers who wanted to know
about his early life that it was his mother's music and religion which
kept the family together. Yet, on a more practical level, it was an
action of Charles Percy's which helped to put the family back on
the road to some kind of economic security, which, in the vast majority of families, at least, contributes to a basic emotional security.

This act came when Percy entered the Christian Science Sunday school class taught by Joseph McNabb, then the president of a small camera company named Bell & Howell. Percy has recalled that after he got to know McNabb, he "asked him if there wasn't some way that a man who wants to work can be put to work doing something worthwhile, something where he can be with his family." McNabb was moved by the teen-ager's argument, for he hired Edward Percy away from his night clerk's job and gave him a job as an accountant with Bell & Howell, in work for which the elder Percy had been trained and which gave him a chance not only to be with his family but also to hold his head up again as a man of affairs.

But nothing is ever acquired without a price being paid for it, and who can measure what it might have cost a teen-ager in emotional stress to intrude into the world of adults, to plead on his father's behalf for a job, and to do so on the implied grounds that it was needed to help keep a family together?

"I know what poverty is," Percy said later. "I have seen how it can pull a family apart." And during the campaign in 1966 he talked in several conversations about the need to pull older people into the mainstream of life, especially older people without adequate funds. He suggested at one point, for example, a scheme tried out in other cities which might be applied to Chicago, whereby those over sixty or sixty-five years could ride public transportation at reduced rates during nonrush hours. He also dwelt, in similar conversations, on the success he had had with enlisting older people in his campaigns, and how much the effort had been appreciated by those whom he had approached.

Much of this also was unquestionably traceable to the example of his mother, an enormously active woman now in her seventies, poring over the shelves in her neighborhood supermarket in Wilmette, playing with the Evanston Symphony Orchestra and even, during the gubernatorial primary campaign in 1964, accompanying her son on trips to entertain political rallies with "Perpetual Motion" on the violin. And also just being the grandmother with a constantly replenished pitcher of lemonade in the refrigerator.

"He wanted a good education," said Elizabeth Percy once. "He didn't express it that way, but he seemed to get a joy out of studying.

He also liked to help other kids; I remember him talking to them on the phone and saying, 'Come on over,' when they had some problem with homework." She was talking then about her son's years at New Trier High School, from which he graduated in 1937, and where, in addition to the other jobs he held for financial gain, he was class president. He also, as a New Trier senior, won a Cook County public-speaking contest. "That was the thing to take in those days," Elizabeth Percy said later. It certainly must have accounted, in part at least, for the absence of regional accent in his voice, the deep tones brought up half-consciously from the diaphragm, the drawn-out vowels and hard-but-not-too-hard-hit consonants.

"I remember him in high school," a former New Trier classmate told a reporter in 1966. "He was always a kind of wheeler-dealer type, a glad-hander. He made a point of knowing as many people in the class as possible. You couldn't resent it, though; at least I couldn't. I was one of the shy ones, and I liked the attention I got from him."

"I liked him a hell of a lot," said another former high school classmate. "He wasn't much of a scholar, but he was popular and didn't come on so strong you pulled away from him. He was sort of the typical Big Man on Campus that you get in a place like New Trier."

In the 1950s and 1960s New Trier High School, which takes its students from one of the highest per-capita income areas in the country, sent more of its graduates to Ivy League and Seven Sisters colleges than any other public high school in the country. Its administrators boast that if an entering freshman wished to take all the courses the school had to offer, it would take more than thirty years to finish them.

A few weeks after he had been elected Senator, Percy came back to New Trier and, in the main auditorium, talked to eight hundred members of the junior class about some of the things he had learned there. He recalled his first day at the school, as a freshman, when a boy sitting next to him had introduced himself and immediately proposed him for home-room president. "From that day on," Percy told the students, "I learned more and more about the advantages for leadership that New Trier provides." He told them—to the accompaniment of laughter—how he had produced a variety show which had lost money, and had learned something from that, too.

And there the students sat, boys and girls, looking very much alike in their scuffed $15 loafers and $30 sweaters, listening to a man who was their neighbor and who had gone the same road they were going, and it was hard to tell whether any of it was getting through or not. He stood before them, neat, perspiring under the hot lights belonging to the school's television station, and he told them about things none of them had ever experienced.

Leadership, he said, as he had learned it at New Trier, meant getting out and doing things for others. He told them how, if you stand still for a couple of minutes in a Chicago tenement, the cockroaches and rats will start climbing over your feet, and how, in the elevators in the high-rise projects, the stench of urine assaults the senses. The leadership they were learning at New Trier, he said, could help provide, among other things, legal help for the impoverished people of the ghetto, twenty miles and an infinite stretch of the human imagination away from the solid creature comforts of the North Shore. Thirty years before, Percy had sat where they were sitting and heard, probably with the same noncommittal, uncommitted expression on his face, another, now-forgotten celebrated graduate of the school. But even thirty years before, when New Trier was not a gigantic sprawling complex—with 3,500 students, now more like a college than a high school—leadership was being drummed into the students.

On his graduation in 1937, it was still a major question whether or not he would go on to college. There was still not enough family money to help out a great deal, although he had been accepted at the University of Chicago, and it was only a few weeks before registration that he learned he had received a scholarship for half his tuition. This was a start, and off he went.

His college career was, academically speaking, something less than distinguished. He passed his examinations, including one course taught by Paul Douglas, although both men professed twenty-eight years later that they could not recall what grade Percy had received. Discreetly, the university declined during the 1966 campaign to disclose the information, possibly for the reason that Percy was by that time a trustee.

It was, however, in other areas that Percy made a mark at the university. He was a strong swimmer and played water polo, serving as captain of the team the year it won the Big Ten championship.

He was also president of his fraternity, Alpha Delta Phi, and class marshal. Until he found his executive feet, he did the usual college jobs, such as waiting on tables and working in the library, but being a salaried hired hand was too slow for a young man who had already been an entrepreneur for a dozen years.

He found that the fraternities were buying their food and having their laundry done individually, dealing with a number of firms. Percy talked the leaders of fifteen out of the college's seventeen fraternities into joining a cooperative movement. The houses had been, for example, paying 7.5 cents a pound for laundry, and a number of laundries were participating. Percy bargained like a rug merchant with a single laundry and got the price down to 3.5 cents. Similarly, with food purchases, the fraternities had been dealing with a number of suppliers, and Percy brought these, too, into a large-scale low-cost buying venture. In both laundry and food buying, he took a fee for himself for organizing and supervising the service. By his senior year, the enterprises were grossing $150,000 a year, and Percy was taking $10,000 for his own share, which, according to university Chancellor Robert Hutchins, made him "the richest boy who ever worked his way through college." Hutchins, who was at the time having his troubles trying to upgrade the University of Chicago's Joe College image into something more intellectually substantial, did not care for Percy's uses of college education for fun and profit. "You're exactly the kind of student I'm trying to keep out of the university," he once told Percy.

At the University of Chicago, Percy also discovered another good money-making proposition. In the late 1960s it is hard to imagine, but during the Depression, colleges—particularly small colleges—were having difficulties finding students. Percy combed lists of various kinds and found names of high school seniors who might be potential freshmen for these colleges. "I got five cents for the name of every senior I obtained and ten dollars if he enrolled in the college," he said later. But the fledgling business executive found an easier way to turn a buck than to go out and find names at a nickel apiece and gamble that they would come in as 200-to-1 long shots. He hired other students to dig out the names for him, paying three cents a name and five dollars per enrollment. "That was the value of being an entrepreneur," he told an interviewer later on.

Much of Percy's profits from the cooperatives and other endeavors went home; in fact, it is a constantly recurring theme in conversations with members of the Percy family about those bright college years that some of the money he made at the university went to pay for his sister's orthodontic treatments.

Young Charles Percy was not a dull boy in college, however. His Alpha Delta Phi fraternity brothers and others remember him in much the same way his New Trier classmates recall him—as social, popular and outgoing, and an indifferent scholar. One incident allegedly revolved around actress Paulette Goddard, who had come to Chicago on a visit to publicize a Cecil B. De Mille film epic called *Northwest Mounted Police*. Percy, on a dare from his Alpha Delta Phi brothers, sought and got a date with the actress, much to the general enjoyment of the fraternity house. Freed from family strictures, he also did some social drinking in college, and recalled once that he had, after a party, written down the names and telephone numbers of girls he had met at the party, but then the next day could not match the names with the numbers.

He gave up the social drinking after college, when he became more serious about Christian Science, but stories about his being a strict teetotaler are somewhat exaggerated. He does, on occasion, take a glass of wine with dinner, and author Theodore H. White, in *The Making of the President 1960*, quoted a Percy associate as saying of him: "When Percy takes a drink of Dubonnet on the rocks, he thinks he's being one hell of a fellow and dissipating like mad." Liquor is kept in the Percy household for guests as well, but, like a great many other nondrinkers of hard liquor, Percy has never been an expert dispenser of drinks. Friends have recalled that a Scotch on the rocks poured by Percy can be lethally generous. "But it's not the kind of house where the fireplace is filled with empty beer cans," a friend once said of the Percys' Kenilworth home, in an attempt to dispel any suspicion that the public image of the nondrinking Percy was at extreme odds with the private reality.

During the 1964 and 1966 campaigns, one of the issues that Percy was constantly poised to answer was whether or not his espousal of Christian Science would somehow hinder him in carrying out the duties of the office.

He was often asked about it in interviews and gave pretty much the same answer to everyone. In 1964, for example, he had this to say:

"It is a logical question: A Christian Scientist does not resort to medicine. Now, there's no law saying you can't. You don't withdraw from the church if you do. And, most important, you don't impose your beliefs on others. But your inclination is not to use medicine, and I never have. I personally believe in the power of prayer. But if someone does not believe in prayer for healing, doesn't choose to follow that route, then my position is he better follow *some* route, and if it is medical care, it better be the best medical care. . . . There is nothing in my religious belief that would hinder me in my performance of the functions of Governor as they relate to the public-health needs of all our people."

In the politics of religion, as was demonstrated during the 1960 election, the only thing about a candidate's church affiliation that makes any difference is precisely what Percy said in the last sentence of his statement—that there was nothing in his beliefs that would hinder him in carrying out the oath of office.

In 1966 he told a reporter that if there had been anything in his religion that would prevent him from doing a job, he would not have been asked to take a high post in the new Department of Health, Education, and Welfare under the Eisenhower administration.

The Christian Science Church is American in concept and has spread throughout the world, with 3,300 branches in 48 countries. It was founded in 1879 by Mary Baker Eddy, who, in 1866, fell on the ice in Lynn, Massachusetts, and suffered what doctors said was a brain concussion and a spinal dislocation. While she was bedridden, she read the account in the Gospel According to St. Matthew of Christ's healing of the paralytic, and wrote: "The healing Truth dawned upon my sense; and the result was that I rose, dressed myself, and ever after was in better health than I had before enjoyed." Even before her accident, however, Mrs. Eddy had been giving close study to the Bible, and as early as 1862, as she wrote (in the third person) in her preface to *Science and Health,* "She began to write down and give to friends the results of her Scriptural study, for the Bible was her sole Teacher; but these compositions were crude—the first steps of a child in the newly discovered world of Spirit."

In her early attempts to promulgate her doctrine of healing through prayer and prayer alone, she said that

> by thousands of well-authenticated cases of healing, she and her students have proved the worth of her teachings. These cases, for the most part, have been abandoned as hopeless by regular medical attendants. Few invalids will turn to God till all physical supports have failed, because there is so little faith in His disposition and power to heal disease.
>
> The divine Principle of healing is proved in the personal experience of any sincere seeker of Truth. Its purpose is good, and its practice is safer and more potent than that of any other sanitary method. The unbiased Christian thought is soonest touched by Truth, and convinced of it.

The Christian Science Church does not have a clergy, and services are conducted by Readers. There is little liturgy and ritual, and for this reason alone, beyond the question of its healing powers, it appeals to many people. It emphasizes a clean, prayerful life in which sin, and therefore sickness, will not hinder the true adherent. "Ours is not a ritualistic church," Percy said in 1967 in an interview. "I don't need ritualization of religion; Christian Science strips religion down to its fundamentals."

And a member of Percy's family said of the Senator: "He likes the ethic of it. That's the main thing."

The tenets of the church require that adherents obey the law of the community, and therefore they permit such things as compulsory preschool vaccinations and inoculations, medical examinations for induction into the armed services or for insurance policies, and having physicians or midwives in attendance where local law requires them. They report contagious diseases and specifically authorize bone-setting by surgeons, where no medication is used, although the booklet *Facts about Christian Science,* an official publication, adds that "there are hundreds of cases on record of serious fractures perfectly healed by reliance on Christian Science alone."

A doctor was called by Percy immediately after he found Valerie in her bed the night she was murdered; so was a Christian Science practitioner, a Scientist with special training in what the church calls "the healing ministry." Neither Percy's spectacles nor his hearing aid violate any concept of his religion. As a trustee of the University of Chicago, he pointed out in 1967, he had voted for the expenditure of millions of dollars in medical research. He is a believer in making Medicare work up to its full efficiency and in state public-health programs.

When it was suggested in 1967 that he might not approve fluoridation of water, he responded that even if he were against it, it was a question of the greatest good for the greatest number and that majority rule should apply. Indeed, he said, he could find no religious objection to it, since fluoride was a mineral, not a drug. If he became President, he told Stephen Hess and David S. Broder in an interview, he thought that the requirements of the office, particularly his responsibility to others, would dictate that he follow the custom of having a full-time White House physician. And he added that he could not think of an instance in which Presidents Johnson, Kennedy or Eisenhower was given medical attention when he might have declined that attention.

"But I've been healthy, my family has been healthy; my parents have been long-lived," he said.

As for his own view toward Christian Science, he said, "I find it a very satisfying thing. It depersonalizes what you are doing, makes it not just a matter of sheer will power, but makes you feel there is a source of guidance and strength you can draw on. There is a sense of optimism about it which appeals to me. Also, it is a wonderfully organized church, and I admire organization. The publications come regularly and are of high quality. I love *The Christian Science Monitor*. It gives you a balanced viewpoint. I've never found them shading an article toward me. They've never endorsed me and never would; but they are wonderfully balanced. . . . An international business-management firm once recommended to the Roman Catholic Church—*Time* wrote about it—that they look at the Christian Science Church as a well-organized, functional business, if you like."

Percy's Christian Science, like George Romney's Mormonism, never became much of an issue in the two campaigns, and an aide said after the 1966 campaign that he could recall only five letters about it. But in Illinois during the two campaigns the talk was there. And Christian Science—in its disciplines, in its ethic, and even in the accidental role it played in throwing his fortunes in with those of Joe McNabb—played a major role in Percy's development.

In the summers, he worked for Bell & Howell, and Joe McNabb, still impressed with his former Sunday school pupil, asked him at the end of the first summer to write a report on the job he had held and to suggest ways it might be improved. "One summer," Percy said later, "I wrote a report showing how the job I was doing could be eliminated altogether by parceling out its functions to other people. The report must have impressed Mr. McNabb, because he asked me not to take any other job after graduation until I had talked to him." Another summer, Percy worked in the customer-service and complaint department and managed to smooth out that operation by devising sixty form letters to answer nearly all complaints. A sample complaint and answer: "I've just taken four rolls of film and they all came out blank." "Dear Madam: Please take off the lens cap."

Percy was not wedded, however, to the idea of going to work for Bell & Howell after graduation. "I had talked to several companies," he said later, "and I had a very good offer from one in particular. I went to Mr. McNabb and told him that I had a great opportunity with another company and that the salary was very generous. 'Whatever the salary is, I'll double it,' he replied. That settled that." McNabb put Percy to work in the summer of 1941, and gave him the job of handling defense contracts, which were beginning to come in as the United States rearmed for what was becoming a nearly inevitable world conflict. In December came the attack on Pearl Harbor and American entry into the war, and defense became Bell & Howell's major business. Percy was given added responsibilities, and added some innovations of his own. For example, Bell & Howell at the time had the reputation of being "the Cadillac of cameras," and most photographers in the armed services were not familiar with the company's equipment. Percy organized and set up schools for military personnel in how to operate and maintain the cameras, including field repairs under conditions that were less than ideal. Before he entered the Navy in February, 1943, McNabb had seen to it that his young protégé was elected a director of the company.

Percy was commissioned an ensign after training at Dartmouth College in Hanover, New Hampshire, and served in Washington, Pensacola, Florida, and Alameda, California, in the Navy's aviation branch. In December, 1945, he was returned to inactive duty as a lieutenant, senior grade, with a letter of commendation in his promotion jacket. His job in the Navy primarily revolved around training aviation units, and he did not go overseas. But while he was stationed at Alameda, attached to the Advanced Base Aviation Training Unit, Rear Admiral V. H. Ragsdale, USN, cited him for his work. The letter of commendation said in part: "The versatility of the NAMT [Ordnance] units, plus the very efficient administration and supervision of those detachments by Lt. (j.g.) C. H. Percy has contributed in a large measure to the training of both squadrons and service units under Commander Fleet Air, Alameda. Lt. (j.g.) Percy is to be commended for his initiative and cooperation."

It was during the war years that Percy suffered a physical setback that plagued him later, to some degree, in business and politics. His hearing became impaired. A Chicago reporter assigned in 1966 to do a profile on the Senate candidate discovered this while interviewing old friends of Percy's; it had not been generally discussed before. When the reporter asked campaign aides about it, he was told that Percy in the 1964 campaign had said that what was described as "a minor impairment" had developed when he was stationed at Pensacola, where his office was at the end of a runway. The noise of aircraft taking off harmed his hearing, the aide said.

But later, when David S. Broder and Stephen Hess were interviewing him for their book, *The Republican Establishment*, Percy said that the impairment had come as a result of the time he spent as a gunnery instructor. In any case, it was not such a serious disability that the Navy had to take official note of it in physical examinations for promotion, but shortly before he went to the Senate, Percy began experimenting with a hearing aid in a pair of glasses. In the Senate chamber itself, the acoustics are not of the best and it is sometimes difficult to hear the speakers even when a Senator is sitting close by. Percy used the hearing aid (the employment of which is not at variance with Christian Science teachings, as spectacles and dentures are not) in the Senate.

In conversation, he prefers to keep his right ear turned toward whomever he is talking with, and, if possible, rides in the left-hand seat of a car. Friends have said that this partial deafness contributed to what was often described as one of his most annoying mannerisms—his interruptions of questions or statements; the truth, according to friends, is that he is inclined to assume that a speaker is finished when he really is not.

During his naval service, Percy married Jeanne Dickerson, a Chicago girl and Northwestern University coed whom he had known for several years. Her father was an engineer and the family owned holdings in a company called Bell & Gossett, now a subsidiary of International Telephone & Telegraph. In later years, there was to be a totally incorrect report that Percy's success at Bell & Howell came because he had "married the boss's daughter." The similarity of their names was the only thing the two companies had in common.

Jeanne was the mother of three children—the twins, Valerie and Sharon, and Roger. When the children were only infants, Jeanne, who was not a Christian Scientist, fell ill and underwent an operation for ulcerative colitis. The surgery was thought for a time to have been successful, but the doctors later recommended a second operation. After that operation, Jeanne was given penicillin and died. Percy agreed to an autopsy and said later that the results had shown that she had died not of the colitis but of a reaction to the drugs. When she died, Jeanne Dickerson Percy was twenty-three and Valerie and Sharon were three. Roger's first birthday fell on the day his mother was buried in 1947.

"She was a very lovely-looking girl," Elizabeth Percy said nineteen years later of her first daughter-in-law. "She was well educated and very bright. After she died, we wanted to help him, especially with the children, but he said he wanted to shoulder this burden on his own. He found a housekeeper and, whenever he could, he would be with the children, even taking them with him on business and vacations."

But on one vacation, a ski trip to Sun Valley two years after Jeanne's death, Percy did not take the children along. Out on the slopes, he met a young California college girl named Loraine Guyer, who was on vacation with friends. "The main thing I remember about him was the way he was dressed," Loraine Percy said later. "He was wearing an old college-letter sweater and a leather jacket. I thought he was a student and I was quite surprised to find out later that he had just been elected president of Bell & Howell."

Percy himself apparently had an eye for masquerade. He told Loraine he was a Good Humor salesman from Chicago, and he had been given the trip to Sun Valley for selling more Good Humor ice-cream bars than any other salesman in the Chicago area. He was invited to join Loraine and her friends for dinner that evening, and Loraine recalled that "he took over the seating arrangements at dinner. I had a date, but Chuck fixed it so that he sat next to me and my date was way down at the end of the table." Executive ability, it seemed, had many applications.

Percy later visited Loraine's family in Pasadena, and it became quite clear to everyone in the Guyer family, a socially prominent Southern California clan which had been highly successful in investment banking, that this young executive from the Midwest was serious about marrying Loraine.

Loraine's father had died a short time before, she said, and besides, "I wasn't at that time really very interested in marrying a man who already had three children." Percy, however, persisted, and found excuses to come to Los Angeles on business and even to pursue Loraine to Europe, where he proposed on a Swiss train and was accepted. David Guyer, the eldest son in the family, told an interviewer that Percy "was determined to do everything the right way. He came to me and asked me, as the male head of the family, for her hand in marriage. I was surprised and in fact a little touched, since he was several years older than I was."

Loraine Guyer and Charles Percy were married in 1950. In 1953 she bore him a daughter, Gail, and two years later, a son, Mark.

CHAPTER 4

Corporate Man to Political Man

In December of 1945, Percy hung up the black, double-breasted suit with the gold lace and gold buttons that he had been wearing for nearly three years and put back on the executive's gray flannel. It was, in a way, almost as if he had never been away from Bell & Howell, except for the fact that on his return he found he had been named corporate secretary of the company. Joe McNabb, who had been described with considerable justice as a benevolent despot, was just as enthusiastic about his young protégé as he had been before Percy went into the Navy. Indeed, the two had kept up a frequent correspondence through the years Percy was away.

But America was changing, and with it the company had to change as well. First, there was a period of readjustment from a war footing to peacetime; like many other manufacturers, Bell & Howell had depended heavily on government contracts, but the government was slicing back hard on those contracts and the consumer had to be wooed all over again. And on top of the readjustment came recession, as the national economy underwent an upheaval in converting from war to peace.

For Percy himself, the period was one of challenge. Bell & Howell was all but dwarfed by Eastman Kodak, the giant of the photographic industry, which, with greater access to mass-production methods, could make a cheaper camera and one that was easier to operate. The smaller company working in this competitive atmosphere had to make sure it had a large enough share of the consumer market to survive. McNabb himself was not sure that radical changes were a good idea, but he encouraged Percy in most of his ideas for marketing and product development, and in 1947 gave Percy to understand that he had, to put it mildly, a real future with the company.

He told Percy that he had written a letter to the board of directors, expressing in the strongest possible terms his desire that on his death Percy be named president of the company. This letter, he said, had been sealed and placed in a safe, with instructions that it be opened only when the board met to choose McNabb's successor. It was, in effect, a "corporate will," and when McNabb died in 1949, the suspense, for Percy, was enormous.

"I tell you, it was *Executive Suite* all over again," Percy told Broder and Hess in an interview. "McNabb's lawyer and I were the only ones who knew about the existence of the letter, and I wasn't sure whether it had been changed since Joe had told me of his plans." But the directors, with an average age in the sixties, chose Percy, as McNabb had wished, over McNabb's son and the other company executives. Percy, then twenty-nine, was not even a vice president of the company. As president, his starting salary was $40,-000 a year, a far cry from the $12 a week he had received when he first went to work for Bell & Howell as a summer employee a dozen years earlier. In addition to the $40,000 salary, there were stock options to enable the Depression-reared young man to become a millionaire by his fortieth birthday.

After he became a Senator, Percy said in an interview that his personal fortune could be "conservatively" estimated at $6 million, the bulk of which was represented by 82,017 shares of Bell & Howell stock worth in 1967 close to $5 million. His annual income from Bell & Howell stock alone was figured at the time to be in the neighborhood of $80,000 a year. These estimates do not include Loraine Percy's own assets from her family's prosperous investment-banking business in Los Angeles. In 1967 Percy put the management of his financial holdings into the hands of Stein, Roe & Farnham, the Chicago investment firm, who were given instructions not to buy shares in companies on which Percy could conceivably exert influence as a United States Senator.

From the outset of his presidency of Bell & Howell, Charles Percy, Corporate Man, was beginning to mix his identity and attention with those of Charles Percy, Emergent Political Being. He had, for example, an intense interest in international trade, based at first not so much on the no-man-is-an-island premise but rather on the premise that, while competition within the camera business might be stiff from Germany and Japan as those defeated countries rebuilt their prewar industries, there would also be markets abroad. Bell & Howell's competitors in the photographic industry were almost to a firm convinced that the only way to beat this competition was to place high tariffs on imports and build their own domestic sales. Percy disagreed and in speeches, at conventions and before Congressional committees fought against the return to high import duties on cameras and other photographic equipment. The Percy view won out.

In the 1950s Bell & Howell even imported, under its own label, Japanese cameras. During the 1964 and 1966 political wars, there were Democratic charges that Bell & Howell and Percy had taken jobs out of Illinois. Percy reacted to the attacks by saying that doing business with the Japanese firms had in point of fact added jobs at Bell & Howell's Illinois plants.

In Percy's seventeen years as a prime mover in the company, two factors helped Bell & Howell to increase its business from $13 million a year to $160 million, its employees from a 1949 figure of slightly over 900 to 10,000, its average employee earnings from $2,000 to $7,500. The two factors were the Affluent Society and the Space Age, and Percy and his top executives, many of whom had been given real responsibility for the first time under his leadership, capitalized on both phenomena. The company made components for photographic equipment used in space exploration, including a lens for a moon-shot vehicle capable of withstanding the enormous changes in temperature on the moon. At the same time, the rise in the American standard of living meant that more and more people were turning to photography as a hobby, and Percy moved with this trend, bringing out a camera—the cheapest in the company's line—for $39.95. A few years before, the cheapest Bell & Howell camera had cost $89. The company made sure, too, that its equipment was competitive in ease of operation. (One nonmechanical member of the Percy family, however, using a competitor's less sophisticated camera on a vacation, quoted Percy as having said: "Even Bell & Howell can't make a camera for an idiot like you.")

Promoting the company's international business also started Percy on foreign travel for something more than tourism. In Asia, Latin America and Europe, he met with businessmen and government officials and began to learn, for the first time, about the problems being faced in other parts of the world. Some of them he found to be similar to American industrial problems. Once, in Budapest, he talked to two young Hungarian production officials who dwelt upon their difficulties in marketing and production and development in highly familiar terms.

"I was flabbergasted," Percy said some time after his return. "Here was a young official of a Communist government talking like an American businessman. I said to him, 'You sound like a graduate of Harvard Business School.' 'Stanford,' he told me. '*He* went to Harvard,' he said, pointing to the other man."

The incident, among others, was transforming a bright but relatively provincial business executive into something larger and more rounded. There were other indicators, too, that Percy was, in business, branching out into fields that were for him new and unexplored. In the late 1950s, for example, Percy and his executive vice president, Peter G. Peterson (who succeeded Percy as president of Bell & Howell in 1964), began to look into the possibility of using television not only for advertising but as a public-service medium. Bell & Howell had already been participating sponsors in such monuments to American culture as "Ellery Queen," "Cimaron City" and "Restless Gun," and the shows had enjoyed reasonably good ratings at relatively low cost. But, as Percy put it, he was "constructively dissatisfied." They had already ventured into the realm of the controversial and nonentertainment television area —in prime evening time with a Chet Huntley documentary on Berlin, with a Howard K. Smith (then at CBS) presentation on the population explosion, which took television for the first time into the arena of the debate over birth control, and with other public-affairs broadcasts, among them a series based on Winston Churchill's hexalogy, *The Second World War*.

In May, 1960, however, they presented the blockbuster in controversial broadcasting, a "CBS Reports" show by Edward R. Murrow and Fred W. Friendly entitled "Who Speaks for the South?"

Percy had been warned that this might be important stuff for the lieges, but that it would result in "boycotts, loss of dealerships and consumer resentment from certain groups."

The history of broadcasting is replete with examples of such warnings to business executives, who then think for a few minutes and pick up a phone to say to a network executive or advertising-agency man, "Look, Jack, about that program . . ." Percy and Peterson listened to the warnings and made their decision to go ahead with the broadcast. A few weeks later, Percy disclosed that a mail count had shown that of 456 letters received only fourteen attacked the company. There was neither a boycott nor a loss in dealerships. The sales for June, the month following the broadcast, were up in the South as well as in the North, and Percy said that some of the letters received pledged undying loyalty to Bell & Howell products on the basis of that single broadcast. Controversy, it seemed, could be good business as well as an act of corporate courage.

Commercially, Bell & Howell was seeking a market which had money to spend, and among the people who had the money were a great many who would watch a Bell & Howell documentary rather than a seal trumpeting "Stars and Stripes Forever" on "The Ed Sullivan Show."

The business community was interested in the Bell & Howell departure, but not much. Before one broadcast was aired, Percy wrote letters to a number of friends who were corporation executives, asking them please to watch the program and to tell him what they thought. The reactions were not altogether favorable, but Robert Lewis Shayon, the *Saturday Review*'s radio and TV critic, quoted one executive who praised the Bell & Howell contribution, even though it was aimed at a minority audience. "If the networks are smart," the executive said, "they'll counteract the Ph.D. crowd who are clamoring for Washington 'to pass a law,' by filling their airlanes with all kinds of educational pap this summer—when viewing is down anyway—so that by fall the masses will be sick of nutritional salads and want a big plate of Western meat and potatoes." This was not exactly a call to the barricades, but it was something.

Another executive thought it poor to use the mass media to try to influence people's thinking, although he did not presumably mention newspaper editorials or mass-circulation magazines, *école de* Henry R. Luce. Still another, however, urged Bell & Howell to "keep trying, because even 'Lassie' on TV is controversial."

Percy, Peterson and other executives had figured that with an annual advertising budget in the neighborhood of one million dollars, it would be senseless to try to compete with the giant corporations—or even the Hallmark greeting-card people. What they could do, and what they did, was to go after a smaller segment, but a segment which could be interested in buying cameras. And the campaign had the effect of selling some cameras, selling the Bell & Howell image and—at least in a broadening area of the business and intellectual world—selling Chuck Percy.

Another aspect of Percy's corporate life at Bell & Howell was knocking the stuffiness out of the company in the minds of the employees and the dealers—and the customers. Percy moved to put the company, which had previously been owned by three families, onto the New York Stock Exchange. More than that, he himself acquired the habit of dropping in on a Bell & Howell dealer in a strange city, inquiring about the product ("How's this new camera selling?" "It's a dog." "Why?" Etc.), and at the end of the conversation introducing himself to the dealer, who was sometimes shocked almost to the point of coronary occlusion but was more often flattered by the personal attention from the company president. Later, back in the executive suite, Percy would find out why the camera was a dog and send copies of the appropriate memos to the dealer, who would, not unnaturally, have a new sense of participation.

The sense of participation also extended to the employees, each one of whom got a handshake and a personal word every Christmas, parties at which corporate education and entertainment were mixed called "Family Nights," and other personal touches in greater or lesser degrees, depending on the employee. Young, up-and-coming executives and plant foremen were more than occasionally summoned for a private chat. "I told these fellows, 'Don't wait twenty years. Tell me what you would do if you were in my chair,'" Percy said.

A former public-relations man for Bell & Howell recalled that Percy was an inveterate author of handwritten notes, which, given Percy's scrawl, often contained more sentimental value than they did decipherable information. The former PR man particularly remembered getting a copy of a release he had written, trying to make a news story out of a highly technical development by the company. As far as Percy was concerned, he had succeeded, and Percy told the man so in a note written across the top of the release.

Any stuffiness adhering to the company's image was also somewhat dispelled by a road-show gimmick in which Percy and three other executives went on a thirty-one-city tour, talking to dealers and salesmen, ending their spiel by putting on wigs, false bosoms and skirts while they mouthed the words to a number recorded by Bing Crosby and the Andrews Sisters.

Percy also put into effect a drive toward diversification in the onetime manufacturer of quality, high-priced cameras, and by the time he retired in 1966 Bell & Howell was not only in the Space Age, but was also selling duplicating machines, mailing systems and other adjuncts of the burgeoning field of automation.

There were some bold corporate moves on Percy's part. With the 1957-58 recession, the day had arrived that everyone in the photographic and allied leisure-activity fields had feared. With an economic squeeze, it was not going to be easy to sell luxury items like cameras. Other companies trimmed development costs; Percy decided to buck the trend. He increased development funds to put new items on the dealers' shelves ahead of schedule. At the same time, he increased the sales budget, driving bargains with television stations and other media to get reductions in rates in return for a larger dollar volume. Profits on individual items were cut, but a mass move to increase sales volume was mounted. The gamble paid off; in 1958 sales were up 15 percent, earnings 22 percent, and Bell & Howell's stock doubled in value.

Some executives who worked with him at Bell & Howell have praised his "qualities of innovation." But innovation is not just coming up with an idea or letting someone else sell you on one; it also means selling the idea to other people—from the company's executive committee to the customers. And it was here, a number of businessmen who knew Percy in the Bell & Howell years have agreed, that Percy excelled. "He's a tremendous salesman," said one close associate, "and his best customer is himself. He takes an idea— his own or someone else's—worries it like a dog worries a bone, and when he's finished, if he likes it, you'd think it was the greatest thing since the wired bra."

In the decade after he took over as Bell & Howell's president, life was for Percy a constant, seemingly never-ending series of successes. Pinnacle after pinnacle—in his business and in his personal life—was reached and conquered. At home, there was the handsome family in the big house in Kenilworth and the family vacations—skiing or Europe or whatever. And for everything there seemed to be a family project. If the vacation was to be in France, by golly, the family struggled at breakfast to speak only French. Percy, superbly organized in business, was an organizer at home as well. When Valerie and Sharon and Roger were old enough, they took turns serving as "captain of the week," responsible, like a chief boatswain's mate, for routing the family out at six-thirty every morning, among other things. Before breakfast, there might be a swim, either in the indoor pool which Percy built alongside the house or, in the summer, in the outdoor pool called Lake Michigan. There was the bond of religion, too, with morning Bible readings and a hymn.

A magazine writer, assigned to do an article on "a day with Chuck Percy" during this period, appeared at the door of "Windward," hangover in hand, at six-thirty one morning. He was brought in, and the first sight that greeted him as he looked out the lakeside picture windows was Percy in swimming trunks, coming up from the beach, drying himself with a towel. There were family prayers and a French-speaking family breakfast, and the writer, recalling the day some years later, said it was "the most depressing goddam sight I ever saw."

The only thing was, however, that the participants seemed to thrive on this regimen, likely because it was not merely organization for its own sake but organization that had something behind it. It would be easy to say that it was love, but that goes almost without saying. Sharon Percy Rockefeller, several years later, for example, remembered one thing in particular about her ordered family life. "Daddy always made sure that whenever any of us were coming home from somewhere, we were met at the plane, no matter what was going on," she said. To love, then, thoughtfulness was added.

So Percy, before he was forty, had reached the Golden Shore. There was, Heaven knew, enough money to go around, to help out others and to participate, primarily because of an exalted economic station, in such endeavors as being a trustee of the University of

Chicago and the California Institute of Technology, a patron of the opera and the symphony—in fact, all the status symbols that a young man from the other side of the economic tracks might want.

But as Bell & Howell grew, so grew Chuck Percy. As he became more and more involved in the world around him, he discovered that he himself was really only half-educated, that a bachelor's degree in economics had not precisely made him privy to the secrets of knowledge in all fields. Politics was one way for him to branch out, to meet people who had ideas other than to become top-flight corporation executives. He had been interested in the Republican party for some time, and had served as a precinct captain in Kenilworth with responsibility for several hundred voters. Being a GOP captain in Kenilworth, however, is rather like being a wine merchant in France; the market is there, it's how you sell it quality merchandise that counts. Because of his business connections, he moved easily into the fund-raising end of Republican politics in Illinois (he was credited with bringing in some $4 million); his moderate bent had made him a champion of Dwight Eisenhower in 1952, and he naturally and gradually began to associate himself with the Ike wing of the party. Besides, an attractive, young, hard-working executive was in demand at the famous Eisenhower White House "stag dinners" and their satellite social-political functions around the country.

But even in this atmosphere he found that there was something lacking. To anyone who had had a brush with Chancellor Hutchins at the University of Chicago, there was the lure of the great books and what lay in them. One day in Pittsburgh, where he had gone for a Republican function, he met a young professor of political science from the University of Chicago, Robert A. Goldwin, a man with a basically conservative turn of mind, who talked with Percy at some length—then and later—about the theory that lay behind the everyday business of the ordering of man's life. For Percy, Goldwin's book learning and philosophy filled a need; the successful pragmatist had to know not just the how but the why. He and Goldwin talked more in the months that followed, and Goldwin was hired, on a more or less regular basis, to come to Kenilworth each Saturday for several hours to conduct a one-student seminar. It was the latter-day fulfillment of the definition of ideal American education—Mark Hopkins on one end of a log and a student on the other.

"He's the only businessman I know who has read all *The Federalist* papers," Goldwin said once. "We used to have assignments—reading that he would do and essays he would write about what he had read—and then we'd talk about the ideas that he had found. At the time, too, he was making a lot of trips back and forth to Washington, both on Republican party business and on Bell & Howell business, and he began to understand a lot of the theory that lay behind the workings of government and politics."

Another Percy associate who was with him in those days with Goldwin said later: "Those talks and those sessions with Goldwin filled a gap in Chuck's approach to the world. He knew that some things happen which shouldn't happen and that other things that should happen don't happen. This told him some of the reasons for things. He knew, for example, that he was a Republican; he'd always been one because his family was. Now he knew what the philosophy behind his thinking really was, that there was, in many instances, a Republican way of getting at a problem and a Democratic way of getting at it. He found out why the two were different and—I think this is even more important—that the Republican way might not always be the best way to go about it."

This simultaneous exposure to the theory and practice of government and politics was turning a pragmatic businessman into a pragmatic political man, and he was, at the same time, being drawn more and more into the national political arena. Eisenhower tried on several occasions to bring him into the government, and once offered him the post of Under Secretary of the relatively new Department of Health, Education, and Welfare. But Percy always refused.

"The General tried to get me to take all kinds of jobs," Percy said later, "big appointive jobs. I told him in 1954 that if he told me he really needed me, I'd do it, but I felt since the people at Bell & Howell had put so much faith in me that I wanted to continue there. I felt that I ought to have twenty-five years in business, but after that I'd go into active politics. I also felt that I wanted to do it the tougher way, not have a chauffeur-driven car and be in an appointive job where I would be supposed to act as if I knew everything."

There was another reason for hesitancy, too.

In recent years the face of American politics has changed so that a man who wants to spend all his time playing the game and playing it well had better have a good chunk of money behind him. If it is his own, he is fortunate indeed. If he does not have a personal fortune, then he sometimes finds himself dependent on others —others who feel they have a call upon him. This is not to say that a poor man need necessarily become, in the old cynical phrase, "the best politician money can buy," but it is a distinct advantage in public life to be serene about your mortgage payments and insurance and endowment policies and how the kids are going to be educated.

For Percy, taking a post in the Eisenhower administration would have meant giving up what he had worked so long to gain— economic security. At Bell & Howell, by the mid-1950s, the programs and policies he was introducing were hitting their full stride, profits and earnings were up and Percy was sharing in the financial rewards. Sticking it out for a few more years would give him the kind of fortune he would need to enter politics on his own terms.

But he was growing restless, too. "I simply found I was reading the political columns of the paper ahead of the business page, and I knew I was hooked," he told an interviewer in 1967. Another family member said he was "just plain getting bored with business." When the job of chairman of the Republican Committee on Program and Progress came along, Percy snapped at it, and jumped with both feet into preparing the report on "Decisions for a Better America." At the outset, however, Percy's enthusiasm almost killed the fragile baby. Into the opening session he brought two University of Chicago professors who attempted some Socratic shock therapy. You can't do what you're being asked to do, they told the politicians and academicians and businessmen gathered for the session. Go home. Forget about the whole thing. The idea, of course, was to stimulate discussion, to bring forth a sense of commitment, and a good idea it was, too, except that this sort of thing usually works better on the campus than it does in a gathering of eagles such as the distinguished Americans who were serving on the committee. "A lot of them didn't know what the hell to think," one participant told Broder and Hess.

But the committee survived and prepared a report which was greeted with loud praise from top Republicans. President Eisenhower said Republicans and other citizens "can benefit greatly by a careful reading of these papers." Vice President Nixon called the Percy report "the most useful and constructive statement of goals and principles ever issued by a political party." And Thruston Morton, then chairman of the Republican National Committee, said the report marked "the first time in history that a political party has deliberately taken a long look into the future to discover what is coming and what must be done about it."

Percy, then, had moved into the upper echelons of Republican theorists and strategists. Eisenhower and Nixon decided he would be, because of his work on "Decisions for a Better America," just the man to be chairman of the Platform Committee when the GOP met in Chicago for the 1960 nominating convention. It took some arm-twisting by Morton to convince Illinois Republican leaders, most of whom were not precisely gleeful at the thought of Percy, the moderate, being in charge of drafting a party platform, but Percy won the post.

"The issues that shaped the Republican Convention were those forced on it by Nelson A. Rockefeller," wrote Theodore White. ". . . For whether he meant to or not, Nelson Rockefeller was summoning the Republican party to repudiate the administration and policies of Dwight D. Eisenhower before the party faced the nation in November." In national defense, particularly, Rockefeller wanted the platform to say that there was an emergency, that Strategic Air Command bases were vulnerable, that the Eisenhower policy of "a bigger bang for a buck" had not been enough and that more effort was needed. The administration, however, was aware that John F. Kennedy, nominated shortly before at Los Angeles, was going to bear down on the "missile gap" and other aspects of the Eisenhower defense posture. And defense was not the only issue. Rockefeller wanted strong language on civil rights, care for the aged, stimulation of venture capital.

Percy, on the other hand, had a 103-member committee composed largely of conservatives who had been given their assignments on the basis of long and faithful party service. Rockefeller's ideas aside, they did not even view the Eisenhower years as a time of achievement according to traditional Republican principles. Percy had to use all his powers of persuasion to achieve a moderately bland platform. Rockefeller threatened a floor fight on the platform if it were not redrafted to reject "Eisenhowerism" and replace it with an even more liberal look at the problems of the nation and the world.

The Nixon forces had thought their Percy-drafted moderate platform, which had been hammered out only with the greatest difficulty over conservative opposition in the committee, was in the bag. They were aghast over the prospects of a floor fight. Percy had shown Rockefeller the draft platform in New York early in July, but had received no commitment. Compromise after compromise was made—a job for which Percy was well suited after his work with the Committee on Program and Progress—but there was still no commitment. As the days dragged on in Chicago, Percy tried to reach Rockefeller or his top aides without result; the Rockefeller strategy at that point was to stand fast and let Nixon come to them if the Vice President wanted to avoid a floor fight. And he would certainly want to; if there were a floor fight over defense and civil rights, it would provide the Democrats with a potent weapon for the campaign.

The deadlock was broken by Nixon. He arranged in secret to meet Rockefeller in New York at the Governor's apartment at 810 Fifth Avenue and, without telling his closest aides, flew to keep his appointment. At midnight, Rockefeller and Nixon arranged a four-way telephone call from Rockefeller's apartment; Nixon sitting at the Governor's desk in his private study, Percy at the Sheraton-Blackstone in Chicago, a Rockefeller aide also in Chicago, and the Governor himself, sitting on his bed in the Manhattan apartment. The talk went on for three hours, and at the end of it Nixon had agreed to what was later known as the Fourteen Point Compact of Fifth Avenue. Stripped of detailed language, it was a sizable surrender by Nixon to Rockefeller, but it accomplished what Nixon had wanted—to move the convention off dead center. To Nixon, the old pro, the platform was of secondary importance anyway; he knew enough about politics to know that a platform means nothing without a man to implement it and the only way to implement a platform is to get that man elected.

But in Chicago Charles Percy was about to be bloodied in national politics.

"No words of pain, outrage and fury can describe the reaction of the Republican Platform Committee" to the news of Nixon's compromise with Rockefeller, White wrote. Barry Goldwater, at a press conference, called the rewriting of the platform "the Munich of the Republican Party," and the Platform Committee agreed. Percy tried every trick in his meager political book to soothe them, but they would not be soothed. Finally, they angrily voted to suspend sessions. Also, from Newport, Rhode Island, where Eisenhower was spending his summer vacation, came a series of messages to the effect that the President regarded the new platform as Rockefeller treachery. Percy, who had demonstrated that he was at best having difficulties holding the Platform Committee in line, was given the job of weaving the Fourteen Points of the Compact into a voice-over narration for a film demonstrating Eisenhower administration achievements—soaring missiles for defense, amber waves of grain for agriculture, happy American faces for civil rights, and the like. He gave up the gavel to Representative Melvin Laird of Wisconsin, a conservative who at least could get a somewhat sympathetic ear from the Platform Committee.

It was Percy's initial, firsthand incursion into the infighting of national politics. Others would have gone back to their comfortable corporate offices and have forsworn any future doings with such bitter and emotional battles. But not Percy.

The staff officer had moved up from the rear-echelon headquarters and had had his first taste of combat. Far from losing his appetite for "the plumèd troop and the big wars," that appetite was whetted.

CHAPTER 5

"Throw Away the Clichés"

"The trouble with Chuck Percy," said a leading Illinois Democrat in the summer of 1966, starting the sentence the way many Illinois Democrats were starting sentences that summer, "is that I don't think he has a real political philosophy. Or if he does, I don't know what it is." The Democrat conceded that Percy had an open mind, but seemed to feel that he had a mind that was so open his brains stood in danger of falling out.

During the course of the campaign, Percy was asked by an interviewer about this observation. "I'll stand, for the most part, on the Republican platform of 1960," the candidate said. "Or better still, 'Decisions for a Better America.' I think that fairly represents my thinking."

"Decisions for a Better America" should indeed represent Percy's political thinking, since he was the chairman of the committee which drafted the document, under the aegis of President Eisenhower, and it was, largely, Percy's idea from the outset.

The project had its beginnings with a call Percy made at the White House in January, 1959, at a time when Eisenhower was preparing his State of the Union Message for Congress. Percy, who was thirty-nine at the time, had a strong pitch to make to the President.

"The nation has moved into a new period of danger, threatened by the rulers of one-third of mankind, for whom the state is everything and the individual significant only as he serves the state,"

Percy later recalled telling the President. "We need a new understanding of the problems, not only to meet a deadly menace and
extend the area of freedom in the world, but also to preserve and
enlarge our liberties."

This was the stuff to give the troops, especially Eisenhower,
who thought in terms of broad political concepts. Eisenhower told
his speech writers to work with Percy's ideas; then a few days later,
standing before a joint session of Congress, the President asked his
audience to "permit me to digress long enough to express something
that is much on my mind," and announced his intention to appoint
a Presidential Commission on National Goals.

To Percy, a short time later, fell the task of doing much the
same thing on a party basis, to become the chairman of a committee which would provide the GOP with a "concise, understandable statement of our party's long-range objectives in all
areas of political responsibility." It was called the Republican Committee on Program and Progress, and between the end of January,
when the committee was appointed, and the end of September,
when it submitted its final report, it had managed to produce a
fifty-thousand-word document which Percy was still inclined, some
seven years later, to call a political philosophy.

"Decisions for a Better America," despite its on-the-one-hand-
this-and-on-the-other-hand-that prose and general approach, is not
an unremarkable document. A camel was once described as a beast
which was planned by a committee, and the committee which
spawned "Decisions for a Better America" was capable of producing
just such an incongruous result. It included moderates like Robert
A. Taft, Jr. of Ohio and conservatives like Stephen C. Shadegg
of Arizona, four years later a top campaign aide to Barry Goldwater. It included Everett Dirksen and labor leaders, Eisenhower's
financial adviser Gabriel Hauge and Representative Charles Hal-
leck of Indiana.

In a lame-duck administration, the committee might have produced a creamed-chicken-and-tapioca dinner for the 1960 campaign.
But it didn't. There is some unfortunate double-talk in the book,
calling, for example, on the GOP to "show a capacity to deal
wisely with the great world and national problems that face us,
while preserving the principles that have given our life meaning
and worth." And sometimes the language appears to tiptoe up to

the water's edge without quite going in. In the area of national security and world peace, for example, the report said that "Republicans stand for the strongest necessary military defense against the threat of tyranny—and for proceeding simultaneously on all fronts with the positive job of helping to bring peace with justice —to ensure dignity and self-respect for all the people of the world."

So far, fairly standard stuff. But the report goes on to say that "we recognize that for the first time America is challenged by a type of war that can be *lost* through military weakness, yet cannot be won through military strength." This sort of statement is, on the face of it, something that probably would not have been put on any record as party dogma a decade earlier since it is a giant step away from the conservative doctrine of *Festung Amerika*.

Neither did the report, despite nearly seven years of Eisenhower nirvana, look at the state of the union through rose-colored glasses. "Performance falls well short of perfection," the committee said and went on to list some of the "tragic gaps" between the American promise and the reality. "There are still people who earnestly seek jobs but cannot find them, people struck down by disease who lack means for decent care," the report said. "There are old people without the simple requirements of a life of dignity; children without access to suitable education; people denied equal rights because of race, religion and national origin. These are blights on the conscience of the most richly endowed of all nations with the means of achieving well-being for its people."

To correct the ills, the authors said:

> We believe:
> That government has a positive responsibility to its people to maintain the conditions for a sound, productive economy. Without this, there can be no opportunity, no assurance of a meaningful life for anyone.
> That every American must have access to the best education his individual endowments enable him to use. To achieve this requires the strongest combined efforts of government on all levels to stimulate the pursuit of excellence in our schools.
> That every American should enjoy every reasonable protection against those conditions or accidents that threaten him with economic disaster through no fault of his own.

In the 1964 Illinois gubernatorial campaign, Charles Percy had help from such members of the GOP pantheon as General Eisenhower...

..and campaigned right down to the vire...

...but drank the loser's bitter draught on Election Night.

Calvin Fentress

On a 1965 Latin-American tour, Percy asked questions and listened to answers in barrios and cities by day...

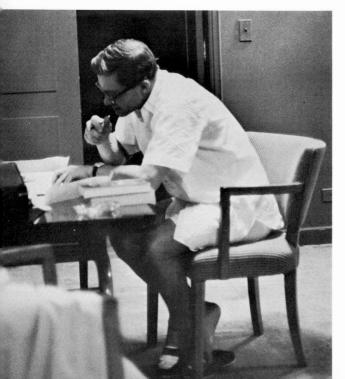

...and spent evenings wri
notes and memos to serv
future foreign policy gu
lines.

Calvin Fentress

In the early 1960s, Berlin's "Wall of Shame" was a latter-day Canterbury for the pilgrim politician.

Campaigning and public life are a family project, sometimes encompassing three generations of Percys. At a 1964 rally, former Vice President Richard Nixon got a handshake of sorts as the candidate's mother, Mrs. Elizabeth Percy, tried to get a word in...

...the candidate greets a captive voter in a barbershop...

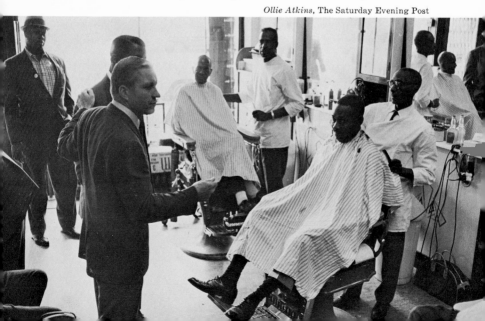

Calvin Fentress

...goes to tenements to talk to children...

...and visits a farm with shirt sleeves rolled...

Ed Reynolds

...and this is the way the day ends—not with a bang but a weary ache all over.

At age six, Charles posed for a family photograph holding his sister Doris as his brother Howard looked on skeptically.

Beside Lake Michigan as a twelve-year-old...

...and as a recruiting-poster ensign, the All-American Boy came through.

*From captain of industry...*At Bell & Howell, Percy made decisions that helped to increase business nearly twelvefold in fifteen years. (His successor, Peter G. Peterson, is at right.)

*...to budding statesman....*United States Senator Charles Percy.

That every American of whatever race or creed must have the chance to make his best contribution to society, to himself and his family and to earn a status of respect.

This was shocking stuff for some Republicans who believed that every man holds, individually, the key to his own destiny, and that if the nation would simply return to the frontier spirit, all would be well. "Our society grows more complicated by the day," the report said.

In an agrarian economy, each family would care for most of its own needs. The advance of industrialization, with its increasing specialization and automation, has steadily increased our interdependence. There are gigantic jobs that only government can do and must do, and others where the government must exert positive leadership and wise cooperation. In identifying those tasks that are properly government's, Lincoln established guidelines:

"The legitimate object of government is to do for a community of people whatever they need to have done, but cannot do *at all*, or cannot *so well* do, for themselves—in their separate and individual capacities. In all that the people can individually do as well for themselves, government ought not to interfere."

Thus far stated, the credo of "Decisions for a Better America" could very nearly have been the credo of the Americans for Democratic Action. The basic problem was that in the body of the report there were statements calling for forthright action in a myriad of fields, but without specific answers to specific questions of how action could be brought about. Furthermore, there were a number of traditional Republican statements setting forth things which should *not* be done rather than suggesting things that should be done.

In the field of foreign policy there were utterances with the same shortcomings. Ringing goals were set forth, then hedged or ringed around with conditions. For example, in a favorite area of Percy's present concern, East-West trade, the report's authors had this to say:

Trade with communist states [the report uses a lower-case "c," apparently lumping all communistic governments as one] should be conducted so that it does not increase their relative military strength. Trade in consumer goods could well stimulate pressure by the Russian people upon their government for an increasing emphasis on domestic production of consumer goods at the expense of military production. Furthermore, trade with satellite nations, if encouraged, has the potential of promoting their independence from Moscow and Peiping.

Our nation stands to gain as our posture becomes more positive in this area. But we should at the same time persist in our requests that they demonstrate their right to the privileges of expanding trade by (1) settling some of their lend-lease and private economic disagreements, (2) providing American companies the same access to USSR producers and consumers as the United States provides the Russian purchasing agency in this country, (3) agreeing to protect patent rights, trademarks and copyrights, (4) placing trade, except for military considerations, on an economic rather than a political basis and accepting neutral rather than Soviet arbitration of trade disputes. The United States should insist on trade conditions that will help thaw the cold war.

During the 1966 Senate campaign, and later in Washington, Percy referred on several occasions to the prospect of putting East-West trade on "a *quid pro quo* basis." While it is difficult to imagine trade being set up on any other basis, he made it clear that he still supported a drive to remove some of the restrictions, but was more flexible. "Let's find out what they want from us and what we want from them and then go ahead on that basis," he said in an interview.

And shortly after his election victory, sitting in his campaign office with one leg hooked over a chair arm, he exhibited a further departure from "Decisions for a Better America." The 1966 GOP successes, he said, were attributable to the fact that "we were for things, not against them. We were for peace in Asia, for housing, for so many things. That's why Ed Brooke won in Massachusetts; that's why Percy won; that's why Mark Hatfield won in Oregon; that's why Bob Taft won in Ohio." But, he added in a paraphrase of Republican orthodoxy, he was not one to match Democratic giveaway programs with GOP handouts.

"I'm going to be in there with a scalpel on some of those federal programs," the new junior Senator said. "The waste and bureaucracy can stand a lot of trimming. But I think that first, as a party, to be respected we have to be respectable. We've got to go after the problems."

In the summer of 1966, when he was stumping the state, he had accepted the clichés and the slogans of "Decisions for a Better America" and the 1960 party platform, the Nelson Rockefeller platform of more or less liberal ideals and ideas. But by December and January of the same winter Percy was moving away from the sloganeering. He had, apparently, begun to develop a political philosophy.

"I'll tell you what it is with Chuck," a close friend of Percy's said one day in the spring of 1967. "In the gubernatorial campaign and in the Senate campaign, he had a lot of half-formed ideas about what ought to be done and how. They were like a lot of splinters floating around. But after he was elected, when no one could touch him, these splinters started hardening, forming themselves into a framework of ideas that he could bounce problems off, bounce solutions off, too. He used to think somewhat along the lines of: 'Here's a solution to a given problem. Is it a good solution from a Republican point of view?' He doesn't do that so much any more. Now he's more inclined to ask himself if the solution is workable within the framework of Chuck Percy's point of view. He *knows* he's a Republican—by background and by general philosophy. He doesn't have to keep turning the pieces around to see if they fit into a philosophical jigsaw puzzle."

The authors of "Decisions for a Better America" saw the role of the federal government as an agency "to stimulate and supplement but not supplant state, local and private action." In 1967 Percy went a step further. Discussing his National Home Ownership Foundation bill, he said that government should play the role of "the innovator, the guarantor." The difference is subtle but significant.

A year after he made the remark that he thought Percy had "no real political philosophy," Percy's Illinois Democratic critic was asked if he had changed his mind. "I think he's got the right instincts," the Democrat said. "And I think he's made a lot of progress. You know, of course, there's nothing like getting elected to give you a sense of serenity. But I think his philosophy is still too broad. He's still too much all things to all men. For example, take a liberal like Clifford Case of New Jersey. And take a conservative like

Roman Hruska of Nebraska. They're both Republican Senators and they're about as far apart as you can get in one party as far as philosophy is concerned. But both of them think Chuck's the greatest thing since night baseball. There's got to be something wrong with a man who appeals to men of such widely divergent philosophies. He hasn't learned yet that you have to make some enemies."

The criticism may be a trifle harsh, since the early favorable conservative and liberal response in the GOP to Percy was to the party salesman, not necessarily to his ideas.

In an interview shortly before he took office, Percy was perhaps more revelatory than he thought when he talked about what he had learned from the elected politicians who had helped him during his campaign.

"I've learned that we've got to throw away the clichés and get at the problems," he said.

CHAPTER 6

Up and Down with
Barry Goldwater

When he ran for Governor of Illinois in 1964, Chuck Percy's major problem was that he was batting with one foot in Barry Goldwater's water bucket. What he later described as his "greatest mistake" was a pledge, taken in 1963, when he started out as an underdog to capture the GOP nomination, to abide by the national convention's choice for President.

Those who were closest to the campaign strategy at the time have the creative memories which politics makes for, but the overwhelming evidence is that Percy's advisers told him, in effect: "Look, you go ahead and take this pledge. It won't make the conservatives mad and they are the ones you have to convince to get the nomination. At the convention, Rockefeller and Goldwater will neutralize each other and we'll end up with someone like Nixon or Scranton. Then you can say, okay, I've gone along with the delegation, now let's get behind the nominee and work for him." Asked once if this had been the general idea behind the pledge, Percy waved a hand and said: "Well, who among us can say what we wished might have been or might not have been?"

Mistake or not, Percy had sworn his oath, and he was going to stand or fall by it, even though fate, by the time the GOP convention in San Francisco rolled around, had put its own hand in. His main opposition for the nomination was Charles Carpentier, a comfortable old Republican pol who had been Secretary of State for Illinois, a man whose signature, in green ink, was in every driver's license. He was known up and down the state as Charles Percy, the Chicago manufacturer, was not. But a few weeks before the primary, Carpentier was stricken with a heart attack and took himself out of the race. Before his death he threw his support to Percy, which made the April primary, despite the conservative opposition of William G. Scott, more or less of a joke. Percy won by a two-to-one majority.

So there was Percy, the Republican candidate, a man with a reputation for being a moderate, stuck with a pledge that by the pre-convention weeks, with Goldwater's front-running an accomplished fact, was rapidly becoming an embarrassment.

"Before the convention," Pennsylvania Governor William W. Scranton said later, "I asked Chuck to support the moderate cause, to join in a stop-Goldwater drive. He told me: 'If there were any way I could get out of this pledge, I'd do it. But I've made it, and I can't see that I can do anything else.'" Indeed, before that, when Scranton was shopping for moderate support, Percy told Mary Scranton, a fighting politician in her own right, that he could not change his mind.

Whatever his reasons and whatever good or harm the pledge would do him, he stayed with it, although for a long time thereafter it soured his relations with the political leaders of the GOP Eastern Establishment. Nelson Rockefeller and Senator Jacob K. Javits, for example, both held Percy in fairly low esteem for his flat refusal to open a branch office for the moderate wing in the Middle West. He was their kind of guy, they had felt, and he let them down.

"He had a chance to be a *Mensch*, a stand-up guy, and he didn't take it," was the way a leading New York Republican official in October, 1967, described Percy's refusal to back the moderates in 1964. Other Eastern Republicans put Percy's action down to naïveté in politics. But the bitterness was understandable, and tagged Percy, long before Michigan Governor George Romney used it publicly in 1967, with the label of "opportunist."

"I was trying to get elected Governor," Percy said later of his decision to stick with his pledge. "I was an amateur and the rest were professionals. I didn't really, I thought at the time, have any business trying to be a kingmaker, a backer of Presidential candidates before the convention picked one."

There were other reasons, too, why the moderates were less than enthusiastic about Percy, the working politician, in 1964. At the convention itself, the moderates felt that Percy, the champion of fair-employment practices in Illinois, was not as active as he might have been in the field of civil rights generally. He was off the convention floor and unreachable when the amendments to the civil-rights plank in the party platform were being offered. And on open housing he said: 'Right now, we aren't ready to force people to accept those they don't want as neighbors. I was for FEPC because there was a consensus in the state for it. There is no such consensus for open housing in Illinois." He wanted open housing by voluntary agreement, not by legislation.

To moderates and to others, the remark was important. What it meant was that, in 1964, Percy was seeking to avail himself of issues which were high in the popular mind; the moral issue of open housing was, apparently, an issue of "force" on people "to accept those they don't want as neighbors." It was, in the view of many, a departure from the corporation executive who had said, consensus or no, to his employees: If you don't want to accept the fact that Bell & Howell is committed to hiring without regard to race from this day forward, you are free to leave. And it hardly echoed Edmund Burke's appraisal, some two hundred years before, of the role of the elected official as a man whose judgment is chosen, not just his ability to parrot the views of his constituency. But for Percy the attitude was very nearly typical of much of his attitude during the entire gubernatorial race.

"Chuck never felt really comfortable during that campaign," a member of the family recalled several years after the fact. "He always seemed to be a prisoner of something—the conservatives who were advising him, his own insecurity about what he was supposed to stand for, something." Whatever it was, Percy was distinctly uncomfortable with his role—and he showed it. While he sort of campaigned for Barry Goldwater, he campaigned more for Chuck Percy. He wore a Goldwater button, but one of the gold variety which required a very close look to determine whose name was on the button in raised letters which were the same color as the background. Reporters from troglodyte Republican newspapers such as the Chicago *Tribune* would ask him questions such as: "Why don't you have a picture of Senator Goldwater in your head-quarters?" He would answer that he did. But if one tried to find it, the picture would hardly be in a distinguished position among the other pictures.

Nor had Percy learned much about stumping the state to gain votes. He depended more on local organizations of Percy volunteers than he did on the county chairmen—a mistake he was not to repeat in 1966—and this did not particularly boost his stock with the regular organization, which did not in any case much care for the idea of a Chicago tycoon running for Governor.

But like him or not, the downstate county chairmen were com-mitted to having him at the top of the statewide ticket, and when he or his campaign strategists canceled or rescheduled appear-ances to suit themselves, the downstaters were, to put it mildly, displeased. Further, the cause of party unity had been hurt by the primary candidacy of Scott. After he had been defeated, Scott had announced that he would support Percy. But in October, John Dreiske, Chicago *Sun-Times* political editor and a man with one of the sharpest political eyes in the country, noted that "in county after county, it was quite obvious that the Scott people were making efforts, and strenuous ones, in behalf of Barry Goldwater but not for Percy." Dreiske said he

found a common response among the primary backers of Scott. Asked if they are backing Percy strongly, the common answer— with a smile—was: "Well, we hope Mr. Percy is elected." The impression was that the most energetic, dedicated and devoted Scott backers would not be too distressed if the November 3rd voting for governor would seem to establish that the Republican party had nominated the wrong man.

Beyond this foot-dragging, which Percy's staff and adherents regarded as disloyalty, since Scott, they said, had promised not to oppose Percy in the primary, was an apparent inability on Percy's part to make himself basically attractive to voters. He had adopted some folksy gimmicks, such as a bus converted into a headquarters in which he and his family toured the county fairs and catfish fries and harness races and night rallies that go to make up Illinois political life.

At bottom, though, it was a combination of factors that mitigated against Percy in those early fall weeks before the election—the now-you-see-it-now-you-don't alliance with Goldwater, the lack of organization support and a forced camaraderie recalling the company president at the office Christmas party. Although he munched corn on the cob until it ran out of his ears and greeted people with a firm handshake and a sincere "I'm Chuck Percy, Republican candidate for Governor, and I'd sure appreciate your vote," he was stiff and diffident, still very much the Chicago businessman. He used statistics "like an IBM machine," he later recalled.

His speeches often were pedestrian, of the sort that could have put a college pep rally to sleep in five minutes. Speaking at a fund-raising dinner in Chicago, he called for more jobs and then said that "something must be done." But he himself did not always seem sure of what that "something" ought to be, aside from creating more jobs and attracting more industry.

Where Percy was strongest in that campaign was in the arena of active politics. The Democratic incumbent, Otto Kerner, had been elected handily four years before after a series of scandals had ripped the Democratic party in Illinois. Percy charged that Kerner, however, was not merely an indifferent Governor, but that he was the tool of the powerful Chicago organization headed by Mayor Richard J. Daley. This is always a popular—and effective—GOP gambit in downstate Illinois, where the voter has a built-in distrust for The City of the Big Shoulders.

Kerner was, Percy said, "a Democratic Governor in Springfield who takes his orders from the Democratic Mayor of Chicago," and that the Democratic party in Illinois "works something like a giant dinosaur; when the head nods in Chicago, the tail wags in Springfield." Downstate and in the Chicago suburbs, this sort of attack—at a Democratic state official through Mayor Daley—has been telling since shortly after Daley was first elected in 1955. But it would be simplistic to suppose that the Mayor, whose Chicago and Cook County constituency and area of influence represent roughly half the state's eleven million population, was some sort of Byzantine oligarch during the 1950s and '60s.

At the core of the Daley organization was organization. From precinct captains through ward and township committeemen, the emphasis was on loyalty up and loyalty down. For business, Daley has provided a clean, well-lighted city, a climate in which most of them could prosper, police and fire departments which worked and other municipal services which were relatively free from corruption and inefficiency. Whether or not it was a democratic form of government, according to the political scientist's strict interpretation, was at least debatable, but the important thing was that it worked.

The proof of the pudding was in the support the organization—"machine" to the opposition—received from the business community and ordinary citizenry in election after election. Many of the same Republican business men who had contracted writer's cramp filling out checks for campaign contributions for Percy and Goldwater in 1964 and 1966 handed Daley like amounts in 1967, and charges by Daley's opponent, John L. Waner, an honest, likable and hard-working contractor, that Daley had wrung "blackmail" from the businessmen fell, for the most part, on deaf ears. Daley was elected, not just handily, but by a margin of more than half a million votes in a city whose total population is only slightly more than three million.

The thought of mounting a campaign against Daley, moreover, was enough to make strong Republicans sob aloud. The Waner campaign cost, by the candidate's own estimate, $150,000—two-thirds of which was his own money. Percy contributed a check for $1,000, a little advice, some staff help and office furniture and one speech at a fund-raising dinner. Curiously enough, the only major Republican figure in the city, state or nation to give substantial aid and comfort to Waner (whose campaign aides often disdained advice) was Governor Romney, for motives that were not substantially clear at the time.

Within the Waner camp, it was felt that Romney hoped to garner some support in future from Chicago's large Polish-American community, to whom Waner was making a major appeal. Romney had already done some impressive spadework in Michigan's Polish-American community. In addition, there could be little disadvantage to Romney in poking Chuck Percy with a stick in Percy's own back yard.

For the first dozen years of its tenure, however, Daley's rule over Chicago was more than mere hard-bitten, impersonal organization, although—and this is what Percy and other Republicans had to fight—the organization was there, registering the voters, ringing the doorbells, pushing the literature and turning out the people every Election Day. The Mayor himself—a portly man of medium height whose relatively infrequent smiles crease his entire face, down to the jowls which make him resemble nothing so much as a friendly bloodhound—is in and out of campaigns, the embodiment of a neighborhood Irish politician; and indeed his whole concept of the city is that of one big, friendly neighborhood like the Bridgeport section back of the Stock Yards where he grew up.

Friday night, March 31, 1967, offered a revealing look into what made Daley and Chicago tick. It was a stinking, cold, rainy night in Bridgeport and Daley was winding up his campaign, as he always did, with a torchlight parade and rally on Halsted Street. Sidewalk amplifiers from music stores blared "Chicago" and "It's a Great Day for the Irish" and competed with the green-jacketed-and-kilted pipe and drum band called the Shannon Rovers, without whose participation no Chicago Democratic do is ever complete. The Rovers skirled and wetly whacked out the songs of Erin—"The Wearing of the Green" and "The Minstrel Boy" and "Garryowen," which, in addition to being Daley's theme, is the familiar, gay staccato phrasing of the U.S. Cavalry's bugle call for the charge.

When Daley spoke, it was in the speech of the Irish neighborhood boy who had made good and who was coming home (he lives only eight blocks from the house where he was born, hears Mass in the church where he took his First Communion). When he spoke that night, it was not of great problems or even great accomplishments, but of people. "I've been blessed," he said, "and the Good Lord has been good to me with steadfast and loyal friends who have stuck with me through good times and bad."

And the times were not always so good. He remembered an election in 1946, "after I was defeated, and I saw my mother and dad, God love them, and they said to me, 'In this life, you no sooner close one door than you open another.' The old people had wonderful advice and wonderful words." He talked, too, about the old days in the neighborhood, and the people he's known—"Some of the oldtimers are here and some of them aren't, God rest them." But if, he said, "we have faith in our neighborhoods, faith in our neighbors, faith in our friends, we can build a greater city. And, by God, we can do it!"

To one of the spectators, who assumed Daley probably would not run again, there was sadness, because that was the last there was ever going to be of this kind of campaigning; the television stations would take it over and the sharp-eyed men with the press releases and the slick slogans and the computers. And when it did go—the families out with all the children and the priests sporting their campaign buttons and the parochial-school bands and the torches— it might be better for the body politic and it might not. But when it did go, to join the ghosts of the "coffin ships" that sailed from the Irish ports a dozen decades ago, a lilt and a magic would have gone with it out of American politics, a touch of the sea-voyaged leprechaun and a touch, too, of the horny hands that carried the hods and built the cities of the New World.

And that's probably the most important part of Richard J. Daley.

As Percy attacked Kerner for being a Trilby to Mayor Daley's Svengali, Kerner was hitting Percy in what many regarded as a soft spot. He was charging that Percy sought the Governor's chair in Springfield merely as "a steppingstone." It was a hard charge to answer, since all that could be done was to deny it; it couldn't be proved. The report, repeated by Kerner and other Democrats up and down the state, did have two offbeat sidelights, however. Houser, his campaign manager, appearing on television in October, was primed to make a denial, if the question came up. He did, too, drawing himself up and assuring the viewers that "the only goal that Chuck Percy has is to be governor of the United States."

"Tom came out to Kenilworth after the show was over," Percy said later. "He walked up the driveway, kicking the gravel, and you've never seen anybody so dejected in your entire life. I said something like 'Thanks, Tom,' trying to make a joke out of it."

As a counterpoint to Houser's gaffe, Norton Kay, political editor for Chicago's *American*, recalls that Percy had earlier made a similar slip in a speech; he talked about "the White House in Springfield" as his campaign target.

The polls, as the campaign went on, showed Percy running well ahead of Goldwater, but a likely loser. The Chicago *Sun-Times* Straw Poll, initiated many years ago, had a reputation for accuracy. In 1964, under the direction of Kenneth Towers, the poll showed Percy trailing by a projected 150,000 to 200,000 votes. When the tallies were in, the final projection would be accurate to within one-tenth of one percent.

Nevertheless, Percy compaigned full tilt, right down to the wire. The day before election, he made a flying trip to eight cities, making airport speeches. In the plane, between stops, he studied the itineraries of twelve other members of his family who were also stumping the state. In the evening, the other members of the family telephoned radio and television stations with "news stories" of what they had been doing during the day, trying to corral each possible uncommitted vote.

On the plane, that election eve, he talked to his traveling companions in tones that were almost desperate. "There must be a lot more I could do," he said, "but frankly, I don't know what it could be." If he lost, he added, the reason would be that "we just didn't try hard enough." Election Day, he voted early in Kenilworth and then crisscrossed Chicago, talking to voters as they approached the polls. But when the votes were counted, he had lost to Kerner by 179,299 votes, but had the pleasure, if that can describe the emotion, of knowing that he did nearly five times better than Goldwater, who trailed President Johnson in Illinois by 890,887 votes.

The conclusion has been termed "inescapable" that had Percy chosen to withhold his support from the national ticket and adopt the posture taken by Rockefeller and Romney, he would have won. But three years later, when the Republicans would be looking around for moderates who were not offensive to conservatives as possible presidential candidates, his name probably would not have been widely mentioned. The view that Percy would have won if he had chosen to oppose Goldwater was widely held in 1966 and 1967 by a number of national political writers and other experts. But those who know Illinois politics better, such as John Dreiske and Norton Kay, maintain that Percy would have lost anyway, and probably by about the same number of votes. They contend that while he would have picked up considerable support from independent voters, he would have been hit extremely hard downstate on the issue of party loyalty and that voters who declared in his favor, even grudgingly, would have deserted him by the tens of thousands.

In any case, following his defeat, Percy did his best to push himself as far away from the Goldwater wing of the party as he could. In December, at a press conference in New York, he said the party had deserved the shellacking it had taken. Moderates, he said, made two basic miscalculations. "Believing that a highly organized minority could never capture the nomination, [the moderate wing] abdicated its responsibility to speak and act. Once the nomination had been won, we thought we could support the national ticket without seriously compromising the party and its future direction." This remark about "abdicating its responsibility" must have sounded a trifle strange to men like Rockefeller, Romney, Scranton, Javits and others who had fought to keep the convention from going to Goldwater.

And he hammered the point home by saying that much of the blame for the defeat belonged to "moderates like me."

The party, he said, "made a critical error because we gave the leadership to men who do not accurately reflect its attitudes and aspirations." The party, he added, "failed the American people" and in future should "work diligently to separate itself from extremist influences. We have not been sufficiently progressive. In many ways, we have not even been soundly conservative. All too often we have been merely negativists, both in word and deed."

Percy also had words for those who were pointing with pride, even in defeat, at the GOP gains in the South. "Our so-called breakthrough in the Deep South is based on an implied if not actually stated rejection of the civil-rights movement. Let us not boast of these inroads, for they are nothing to be proud of. It will take a prodigious and sustained effort if we are to recover the confidence of the American Negro and citizens devoted to civil liberties and civil rights."

As a first step, he said, he suggested a change in command in the national GOP organization, with a panel of leaders shaping policies while others carried them out. He did not, in his New York statement, call for the resignation of National Chairman Dean Burch, but the next day in Washington he met Burch for breakfast and suggested that it might be in the interests of party unity if the chairman, who had been picked by Goldwater, step aside.

So the 1964 campaign was history, and Percy was striving to rebuild his moderate image after it had become slightly shop-soiled through his support, albeit lukewarm, of Goldwater and the Illinois conservatives.

CHAPTER 7

Toward the Senate Race

There have been observers of the Percy phenomenon, such as Garry Wills writing in *The National Review,* who have said that Percy's penchant for "problem-solving" often results in a solution being found for Chuck Percy's particular problem rather than for the community's, although some help is usually rendered to the community at the same time. Through 1965, the New Illinois Committee managed to keep body (Percy) and soul (enthusiasm for the Percy future) relatively intact. More important, it began to introduce Percy's name more and more into the ghetto on a voter level.

"On the day after the election," Percy recalled later. "I woke up and I got to thinking that here we had all these campaign goals and why don't we try to see what can be done with them through private—not public—methods, how many of these goals can be achieved even though we lost the election?" Backed by private money and staffed by both professionals and volunteers, the New Illinois Committee ("NICOM" to the initiated) was formed.

At the heart of NICOM was "Call for Action," by which citizens with complaints about landlords, about city departments, about merchants, could call 346-6667 in Chicago and have their complaints recorded and worked on. The caller was greeted with a recorded message in a familiar voice: "This is Call for Action, Chuck Percy speaking." Then Percy would advise the caller to stay on the line and put his complaint, along with name, address and telephone number, onto a tape. After that it would be worked on by the NICOM staff.

"Call for Action" and the "New Illinois Committee" had nice, statewide rings to them, but they were primarily tailored to the ghettos of Chicago, despite Percy's joking boast later that "Call" had helped a woman living in a plush Gold Coast lake-front apartment house in a dispute with her landlord. NICOM leaned on city departments and claimed results in such areas as rent reductions, rat and roach infestation, trash removal, welfare-check processing. In addition, classes staffed by volunteers helped rehabilitate functional illiterates to remove them from welfare rolls. By the fall of 1967, "Chuck Percy speaking . . ." had been replaced by "Senator Percy's Call for Action . . ." when 346-6667 was dialed, and NICOM was deep into such matters as studying ways of giving technical aid to Negro small businessmen, to build their stake in the economy of the ghetto.

According to the research of the Chicago Urban League, there was in 1967 only one Negro-owned manufacturing firm employing more than three hundred people; most of the rest of the Negro-owned businesses were what are described in New York's Jewish community as "poppa-mamma stores," whose owners and operators eke out a precarious, marginal existence. For the balance of the ghetto business community, it is what economists call a "drainage economy"; the money is made outside the ghetto, is spent in the ghetto in the form of rent and retail goods and services and then taken outside the ghetto again.

Despite its record for having more Negro-owned businesses in the ghetto than any other large American urban community, Chicago is still a haven for entrepreneurs who charge high prices for inferior food, as well as for slum landlords and rapacious installment-plan salesmen.

NICOM and Percy, banners high, set out to cure some of these problems, and they did help, but NICOM, for all the faith that some of its "business-can-do-it-better-than-government" proponents liked to place in it, never had a very high score on the pragmatic scale.

Its mission, whether intended or not, was larger. It introduced Percy's name to the ghetto on a mass basis.

On a wider horizon, Percy's financial backers, such as Clement

Stone, Chicago philanthropist and Percy supporter, were kept on the string and not allowed even to begin to think that Percy might be through as a force in Illinois politics. NICOM was avowedly formed "to pursue those goals and activate those programs outlined in 'the new Illinois' that Chuck Percy has envisioned." Some of the campaign staff was kept on, working on "pursuing those goals." New recruits, professing an interest in Percy, were inspanned to work for NICOM rather than to wait to see what the political future might bring.

On an even wider horizon, one group at NICOM was set to work writing research reports on the U.S. commitment in Vietnam, indicating an awakening interest in the possibility that it might be better to run for the Senate in 1966 rather than wait, as a once-defeated candidate, to take another crack at the gubernatorial chair in 1968.

There were, however, deep divisions among Percy's strongest supporters on making the race. One group, particularly Tom Houser and H. G. (Skinny) Taylor, held the opinion that it was senseless to take the risk of being beaten by a strong opponent like Paul Douglas, that it would be better for Percy to bide his time and rebuild his fences and try to win the Governor's chair in 1968. Part of this group which wanted Percy to wait also felt that there was considerable pressure being applied by conservatives to have Percy run for the Senate and that this pressure should be well evaluated before any decision was made.

Percy had annoyed, and in some cases angered, conservatives in 1964, and the wounds were not healed. His ho-hum support of Barry Goldwater, his high-handed individualistic methods of campaigning, his moderate-to-liberal philosophies still rankled. The conservatives, or at least some of them, believed that by running Percy for the Senate they would have nothing to lose. If he won, he would be in Washington where a junior Senator—especially a junior Senator from a state where Everett McKinley Dirksen was the senior Senator—would have only small crumbs from the patronage pie and would be a long way from the center of Illinois politics. If he lost, well, then, as one conservative put it in 1967, "It would have been a question of 'wave bye-bye to the nice man.'"

Through the summer and fall of 1965, the debate continued, inside and outside of the Percy camp. The GOP state chairman, Victor

Smith, was eager for Percy to make the race; so was Mrs. Audrey Peak, the national committeewoman.

Outside of the Percy camp and outside of Illinois, there were rumblings that 1966 might be a Republican year, or a year, at least, in which the candidacies of people of the Percy stripe would fare better than they had in 1964, when Goldwater was not an issue, but *the* issue, in a great many races. There were still questions, however. How far had the Goldwater ghost been exorcised from Republican circles? Was there now beginning to form a sincere desire on the part of GOP politicians to win in 1966, rather than go through another political purification rite such as the country had seen in 1964?

There were some important races to be watched in 1965, particularly that which John V. Lindsay, a forty-three-year-old Republican urbanist, was making in New York against an entrenched Democratic party. Lindsay and Percy were, on the exterior at least, cut from the same bolt of cloth. Through "Call for Action" and NICOM, Percy had taken an awakened interest in the cities and the vast Negro vote which was beginning to stir there. Besides, there were other trends. All across the country, young, well-educated independents were marrying and leaving the cities for the suburbs, which were becoming new party battlegrounds. The war in Vietnam was turning from a scrimmage for professional soldiers into a full-scale conflict, and the term "credibility gap" was more often and more loudly heard. At home, the civil-rights struggle was moving from the rural South into the cities of the North, from a crusade with a religious base and a religious intensity into a raw struggle for power, within the movement and outside of it. "Black Power" and "white backlash" were smoldering issues.

For Percy, the decision would be monumental, and, as shown in the subsequent campaign, it would be an all-or-nothing gamble. Broder and Hess, in *The Republican Establishment*, put it this way: Like his decision to run for Governor against Charles Carpentier in 1963, "his decision to run for the Senate in 1966 was an incredibly risky one. It was the sort of choice that only foolhardy politicians or men of driving ambition make—the same sort of decision that sent John Kennedy into West Virginia in 1960 and Richard Nixon into California in 1962."

In the meantime, the pressure on Percy kept mounting. One of the major factors which pushed him toward his decision was the appearance in Kenilworth one night in November, 1965, of Richard B. Ogilvie, who three years before had won the Cook County sheriff's office on a racket-busting campaign platform. Ogilvie had made a good record in his term, although it would be difficult for a reformer to do otherwise. It had been said in the less tasty days of Chicago politics that the sheriff's office was a sort of preretirement fattening pen, that a man could make enough in graft and favors to be able to live out his years comfortably. Ogilvie, who a few years before in his thirties had made a name for himself as a federal prosecutor of the Thomas E. Dewey school, was now considering running for the presidency of the Cook County Board, which carried with it some twelve thousand patronage jobs—a juicy plum for the power-starved GOP ward and township comitteemen.

"Ogilvie told me, 'If you don't run, I won't run either,'" Percy recalled later. "He said that if the head of the ticket wasn't strong, the whole Republican campaign was likely to be a slaughter."

So the meetings started again with top Illinois Republicans, reassessing Percy's chances and taking a harder look at the issues. One thing which bothered Percy was what role Dirksen might be expected to take in the campaign and whether, as a major spokesman for GOP conservatism in Illinois and elsewhere, Dirksen might attempt to throw cold water on some of Percy's most cherished issues and thus rob them of some of their spark with the voters. Moreover, Percy was worried lest Dirksen and he might be viewed as the Gold Dust Twins in the Senate, with Percy slavishly following Dirksen's lead on voting.

At a meeting in Chicago in mid-December, 1965, just two days before Percy announced his candidacy, he extracted from Dirksen a letter which gave him independence of action, both as a candidate and by extension as a United States Senator.

Dirksen said he recognized that "from time to time we may feel differently on some issues and I respect this right on his part." The senior Senator also acknowledged that he and Percy had worked closely in the past on a number of party projects, and closed by saying, "I know that we are in accord on the historic progressive principles of Republicanism."

It was a peculiar political document. It was obvious that Dirksen, as the ranking GOP officeholder in Illinois, would support Percy at least tacitly. It was equally obvious that the two men reflected two differing viewpoints within the Republican philosophical framework. But these differing viewpoints had been held by others in other states without permanent damage being done to the party. The political reasons why Percy insisted on this manumission from Dirksen have continued to puzzle students of Illinois politics long after the fact.

Dirksen also had long been aware of what he considered another side of Percy. In 1962 Percy had an appointment with President Kennedy at the White House to talk about reciprocal-trade legislation. At the end of the interview, apparently intrigued by the eager attention to detail and delivery which Percy had shown, and very possibly with the politician's eye for a fellow professional, the President asked Percy what his political intentions were. The answer was vintage Percy: "One of the exciting things about the future, Mr. President, is that none of us can really prescribe what will happen to our lives."

Later, Kennedy pressed Dirksen, as the two of them were walking in the White House garden, on what Dirksen thought Percy's goals were.

For answer, the GOP Senate leader smiled, raised a long finger and pointed to the doors of the Presidential office.

The areas of disagreement between Percy and Dirksen did not strike precisely at the roots of the Republic. Percy wanted expanded East-West trade, Dirksen didn't. In addition, they differed on the school-prayer amendment; Dirksen sought Congressional action to override the Supreme Court decision outlawing prayer in public schools, Percy felt it was a matter for individuals to decide. Another, less important area was Section 14-B of the Taft-Hartley Act—the "right-to-work" clause, with Dirksen favoring stiff laws to outlaw the closed shop and Percy taking a less extreme position.

At this point in time, too, Percy was beginning to shift his position on legislative reapportionment. In 1964, just after the "one-man-one-vote" decision of the Supreme Court, he had attacked Democratic candidates who had hailed the decision. Percy called the ruling "an erroneous and simple-minded view" of the machinery of government. At the county fair in Kankakee in 1964, he spelled out his views more precisely, telling his audience that the decision "denies the fact that, in addition to the fundamental principle of majority rule, there are other considerations which contribute to equal representation of the people." He said he "enthusiastically" endorsed the constitutional amendment sponsored by Dirksen which would reverse the ruling.

But later, after his defeat, he began to move away from this position. He was asked, for example, what his views would be if Dirksen, who had failed in his attempt to push the amendment through the Congress, brought it up again. "I will study it with an open mind," Percy said.

In the Senatorial campaign, these shifts in position were to hurt, but not mortally. When Douglas attacked him for changing his ground on reapportionment, Percy replied, perhaps a trifle smugly, that he expected to change his mind any time he became convinced that a previous position he had taken was wrong. Douglas countered with one of the more quotable quotes of the campaign, charging that his Republican opponent had "raised vacillation to the level of high moral principle."

At the root of many of these difficulties was an attempt on Percy's part to be with, but not of, the Dirksen wing of the party in Illinois. But more basic was the growing realization that the conservative arguments he had used in 1964 no longer held good in 1966, that he must move closer to his opponent's liberal record—indeed, to show that he was a younger, better Paul Douglas and that he deserved the voters' support for that reason.

But the real troubles with Dirksen were not to start until after he was elected to the Senate, and they were to come on a much more serious matter—Vietnam.

CHAPTER 8

Paul Douglas:
Giant in the Earth

The late Edward R. Murrow once described Winston Churchill's role in the pre-1940 days in the House of Commons as that of "the conscience of England." For nearly eighteen years, Paul Howard Douglas, rimed and craggy as the granite rocks of his native Maine, had sat in the United States Senate, playing much the same role as that which Churchill had played, warning of rocks and shoals ahead and forging legislation and programs to avert them.

For a dozen years before that, he had played a similar part in Chicago politics, a maverick member of the City Council elected from his own peculiar constituency in the Hyde Park area around the University of Chicago, an eyrie for eggheads. In the days on the City Council, and long afterward, his heroes were Fighting Bob La Follette, whose Populist views of America presaged the New Deal and the New Frontier; Jane Addams, who held the heretical notion that poor people ought to be helped to widen their own horizons and not just fed and clothed; John Peter Altgeld, the Illinois Governor who believed that justice was important even when unpopular; Clarence Darrow, the criminal lawyer who was a philosophical disciple of Altgeld.

Douglas did not number among his heroes "Boss Ed" Kelly, undisputed ruler of Chicago politics, nor any of his cohorts, and the feeling was mutual. But the experience did him good. The economics professor found himself with a solid grounding in practical politics learned in a rough school. It taught him, too, a lesson that stood him in good stead both in politics and in combat as a Marine officer: that when the "incoming mail"—political or military—starts exploding, the thing to do is to scrunch down a little farther in the foxhole, pull the helmet chin-strap a little tighter and wait it out. When it's over, the time will be ripe for a counterattack. Douglas survived the political barrages as he did those on Peleliu and Okinawa; his wounds bloodied him but slowed him down not a whit.

In 1942 he tried for the Senate nomination and the Kelly machine knocked his brains out. The next day, Paul Douglas, Quaker and former pacifist who had failed a physical examination to enlist in World War I, put his affairs in order and started pulling strings to get into the U.S. Marine Corps at the age of fifty. An old Chicago friend, Frank Knox, was Secretary of the Navy and at Douglas' insistence, the physical and age requirements were waived and he went off to the Marine Corps's Recruit Depot at Parris Island, a "boot" of the rear rank. In 1945, as the Marines were fighting on Okinawa, Douglas, by then a staff officer, had his left arm nearly shot off by Japanese machine-gun bullets. It still is of little use to him—"except as a paperweight," he has said.

By 1948 he had returned to the political wars, and won the grudging blessing of the Democratic organization to run against Senator C. Wayland (Curly) Brooks, the Republican incumbent. In that summer and fall of 1948, the year that was supposed to be impossible for a Democrat to be elected, Paul Douglas began to forge the campaigning style that was to send him to office in November and to re-elect him twice. He was nearly professorial in approach, larding his speeches with literary allusions and literate jokes. But more important, he built up a widening circle of political friends and debtors—county chairmen, township committeemen, state legislators, union leaders and rank-and-filers. In his last campaign, a long-time political writer said of him that he "knows every single Democratic politician in every town in the state with more than two thousand people living in it."

When he got to the Senate in January, however, it looked for a time as if it were to be the Chicago City Council all over again. He was a loner, a backwoodsman from the Groves of Academe, a man who shunned power in an atmosphere of "the world's most exclusive gentleman's club." And what wild, radical notions he had for his fellow Senators in those early years! He believed, for example, that Negroes were entitled to equal rights and that these rights ought to be secured by federal legislation; he believed that the land belonged to the people and that it was up to the federal government to see to it that it was kept green and open and undeveloped so that future generations could enjoy it; he believed the federal government should take a hand in keeping air and water clean and unpolluted.

There were other ideas, too. The professor of economics was put to work as soon as he had arrived in the Senate to hammer out some federal formula to meet the problem of rising costs of living due in large part to a policy of excessively low interest rates. Douglas was named chairman of a special new subcommittee of the Joint Economic Committee and, after a study, the committee recommended that money management, both by the Treasury and the Federal Reserve, be keyed to what effect it would have on purchasing power, jobs and production. In addition and even more important, Douglas proposed that primary power be vested in the Federal Reserve System and that Treasury actions be consistent with Federal Reserve powers. The accord, the working partnership between Treasury and Federal Reserve, was later hailed as giving the federal government, for the first time in years, an effective monetary policy —one which could simultaneously stimulate economic growth and also hold down prices.

In his first year in the Senate, too, he wrote the first slum-clearance and urban-renewal bill. It became law in 1949, and later, as a member of the Senate Banking and Currency Committee, he wrote and pushed through amendments to the original bill to strengthen it, widen it, make it more effective. Through the 1950s Douglas proposed civil-rights legislation, particularly in the areas of equal voting rights and equal rights in jury trials. He was a leader in the fight to pass the 1957 Civil Rights Act, the first such federal legislation to be passed by the Senate in eighty years, and he was the chief sponsor of both the 1960 and 1964 Civil Rights Acts. At the same time, he fought to prevent filibustering civil-rights bills to death.

Not all the legislation he proposed was successful; much of it died in committee in those early years. Mary McGrory, who graces the craft of journalism on the Washington *Star* and other papers, related after his defeat a typical Douglas reaction to setback. One day in 1956, she wrote, Douglas

> hurried over to the House to intercept a civil-rights bill which had just passed. He hoped to prevent it from falling into the wrong hands, but the House messenger passed him with what he later called "jet-age speed" in the hall, and when he came back, the bill had already been referred by the presiding officer of the Senate, Lister Hill of Alabama, to the Judiciary Committee, where sudden death awaited it.
>
> Some days later, Douglas tried to get the bill out of committee. [Democratic leader Lyndon] Johnson brought the matter to a vote and Douglas was one of six who stood up on the affirmative side.
>
> He was crushed that day. An aide remembers him walking to the elevator and saying, "Push the button three times and let's pretend we are Senators."

In the midst of defeat, discouragement and disappointment, there was time for a wry joke. But it wasn't all defeat, although the battles tended to be long, the foe refractory. Medicare, in which Douglas was an initiating force, took five years to become law; federal aid to education, especially teachers' salaries, financed out of offshore revenues, took twelve years; liberalization of immigration laws took another twelve, with victory coming only in 1965; voting rights, which he fought for in partnership with Hubert Horatio Humphrey, took five years.

When it came to debate, Douglas had the reputation of a killer of bad legislation on the floor of the Senate. In the last session in which he was a member of the Senate, he successfully led the fight against what his Democratic Senate colleague, William Proxmire of Wisconsin, called "those one-man, ten-vote amendments" which would have overturned or limited the 1964 Supreme Court decision calling for state legislatures to be apportioned on the basis of one man, one vote. Senate Democrats also credit Douglas with saving consumers of natural gas upwards of $600 million a year by his fight against a price rise. There were other battles in behalf of consumers, including the "truth-in-packaging" bill, which was passed by the Senate in 1966 and was a foot in the door against mislabeling, as Douglas put it during his last campaign, of "giant-sized quarts" and "jumbo pints."

Some of his efforts were dubbed "treasury raids" and "federal interference in the rights of free enterprise." The former Socialist was often assumed by his adversaries to be an exponent of increased government spending, but there was a streak of thrift in him, due, according to myth, to his Scots ancestry, but in truth more probably a result of his upbringing in the harsh rural life of Maine, where care for a dollar is not particularly a virtue but a condition of life. In fiscal 1965, for example, he was given credit by Defense Secretary Robert McNamara for saving the taxpayers some $4.8 billion through his subcommittee's examination of defense procurement and cost-accounting procedures. There was a plan to build a parking garage under Capitol Plaza in Washington, which Douglas successfully opposed at an estimated saving of $50 million; there was his fight to require competitive bidding on contracts for shipping military goods on private carriers; there was his winning fight to block tax deductions for self-employed voluntary pension plans.

Paul Douglas, with his affinity for Congressional giants of the stripe of La Follette, George Norris and Robert Taft, was destined, however, to serve for six of his eighteen years in the Senate under the leadership of a man who believed primarily in leadership, not open discussion of the issues. The man was, of course, Lyndon Baines Johnson of Texas, and his philosophy of the method by which the Senate should operate was vastly different from that of Douglas. Once, during the Eighty-fourth Congress, the Democratic leadership was able to pass more than a hundred bills—and not all of them noncontroversial—in less than an hour. The reason was simple: the word was passed that "Lyndon wants it." The Douglas approach, that "the country needs it," took more time, and often tended, because of Douglas' stubbornness, to leave Douglas out in the cold, or at least in the "outer circle" of influence. That the particular circle which Douglas inhabited was less Dantean than might be supposed was more due to his own powers of persuasion in committee and in floor debate than to his adherence to the Senate system. Johnson, superb legislative engineer that he was on Capitol Hill, was inclined to believe debate unnecessary in most instances; what really counted was the sculpture worked on a bill in committee, the consensus.

Indeed, after Douglas left the Senate, a chief mourner was an archadversary, his fellow Illinoisan, Everett McKinley Dirksen, who made no secret after Percy's election that while he welcomed a second Republican from Illinois, the departure of Douglas left no foe worthy of Dirksen's debating steel on the other side of the aisle.

Douglas, during his years under Johnson's leadership, often chafed in the harness, and was inclined to buck and crow-hop to throw it off. Once, after an intraparty battle over the form and substance of the Area Redevelopment bill, Johnson came over to Douglas' desk to congratulate the Senator who had won, but who had given the Democratic leadership so much trouble while he was winning. "With your parliamentary skill and my program, Lyndon," Douglas told Johnson, "we could go a long way."

But while Douglas was having his problems with Johnson and with the Republicans, another, younger Senator was listening. He was John F. Kennedy of Massachusetts, and he was taken not only with the Illinois Senator's fighting spirit and talent for eloquence, but also with his theories of how economic growth for the nation could best be achieved. After Kennedy was elected President, life in the Senate became a little easier for Douglas. He did not win any powerful chairmanships; Kennedy's influence did not extend as far as to be able to twist arms of senior Senators. But his programs and plans found a more sympathetic ear with the White House than they had with the previous Democratic leadership, which, after all, had been trying to survive under a Republican administration. Paul Douglas was less lonely.

All this, however, was the Washington Douglas. Where did his voting strength lie in Illinois for all those years? In general, the support fell into five groupings, some of which merge and some of which are firmly and clearly outlined.

First, he had a strong attraction for the intellectual community which abounds in Chicago and the suburbs of Cook County, as well as pockets downstate, such as in the community around Champaign-Urbana, home of the University of Illinois.

More important in numbers were the labor unions, whose rank and file were devoted to Douglas, although he sometimes differed with their leadership. Next came the two numerically strongest minority groups, the Negroes and Jews of Chicago and its suburbs. Fifth, also strong in Cook County, were the so-called "ethnic groups" of Cook County, the descendants of immigrants from Eastern and

Central Europe—Poles, Ukrainians, Bohemians, Hungarians, Slovaks and others.

These five groups, in general, permitted Douglas to come out of Cook County in any election with a plurality of several hundred thousand votes, more than enough to offset the downstate Republicans. But even downstate, aside from the intellectuals of the university towns, the Negroes of the Illinois suburbs of St. Louis and the union members in the industrial towns, ever growing in number in once-rural Illinois, Douglas had a "cash register" full of votes which he had carefully cultivated through the years: the Populist strains among the voters—marginal farmers and small businessmen in the towns who responded to his constant trumpeting against the "special interests."

It was indeed an odd combination of strength and virtues, of attributes and attitudes, that managed to hold together these diverse groups for eighteen years. To conservative Democrats in Chicago, vestigial remnants of a more colorful if less enlightened political era, Paul Douglas was always "the Perfesser," a figure of fun, perhaps, but a man to be worked for every six years when the powerful city and county Democratic organization said "Work." But even back in the days when he sat as a maverick member of the City Council, he was listened to and respected for his views. Mayor Kelly, for example, puzzled Douglas; the Mayor was always outgoing and pleasant to him even though Douglas consistently opposed him. Douglas once asked Kelly why this should be.

"Don't give it a thought," Kelly replied. "You'll never realize what a friend of mine you are. When these pirates get too greedy and come to me with their schemes, I'm able to say, 'Now what do you suppose the Perfesser would say about that?' That usually does it."

So even in his earliest, least effective days as an elected politician, Douglas was a conscience to the body he sat in. But a man would find it difficult anywhere to be a conscience for anyone unless he had a pretty good one of his own, and Douglas' conscience was forged in a crucible of white-hot self-examination that often took him into unpopular causes. In World War I he was a pacifist while a student at Bowdoin College in Maine. He opposed American entry into that war because, as he said, "I believed human life was sacred and should not be taken by human hands."

And yet, years later, he and his wife Emily, daughter of sculptor Lorado Taft, visited Italy and saw Benito Mussolini's Fascists at work with their own eyes. "I will never forget," he said, "sitting in a cheap boardinghouse in Ravenna, after a long third-class train ride on a rainy night, when it suddenly became clear to Emily and me that armed resistance and a terrible war would be the inevitable end of it all." From that point on, he believed, although with often sinking heart, that armed might was necessary to deter aggression, that wars, when they must be fought, should be vigorously prosecuted. Long before his last campaign, when his proadministration stance on Vietnam was an issue, Douglas was attacked by liberals for his cold-warrior views. But he was never attacked for his lack of integrity; it would have taken a brave liberal indeed to choose that road.

During the Korean War, shortly before the Chinese Communists jumped the United Nations forces at the Yalu River, Douglas had this to say on the University of Chicago Round Table: "We have not used the atom bomb on Russia. But I would say that our patience is not unlimited. I would say that at the next act of aggression by a satellite against the peace of the world, we should strike at the eye of the octopus which is trying to control the world. . . . If necessary, we should even consider using the atom bomb against mainland China. But I would prefer to use it against military formations in advance of our troops."

Douglas' reply to attacks on statements such as these were consistent; he maintained that the true liberal supports the thesis that freedom is impossible and decency cannot exist in a police state. "The Athenians did well," Douglas told the graduating class at Amherst College in 1966, "to make the owl and the olive tree their symbols to denote wisdom and peace. But freedom tempered with love is the only atmosphere in which true wisdom and peace can flourish. And to preserve and maintain all these virtues, a strong admixture of Spartan courage is needed. Thermopylae was necessary that Socrates might practice his dialectic."

On domestic issues, too, Douglas was quick to follow his conscience where it led him. When he arrived in Chicago in 1920, he joined the Society of Friends because of their pacifist views, because, as he said long afterward, "I believed, and still do, in the effective power of organized love and goodwill. The Quakers have helped me to be a better man." He also was a Socialist, and his hope for organized love and goodwill did not stop him, one evening, from taking a group of his students down to the South Chicago mills to organize the steelworkers. The police sowed less than goodwill, and the invaders from Hyde Park were put into cars and deposited far from public transport in the countryside.

His relations with Richard Daley were, in the early days of their association in the 1950s, when Daley was county chairman, more or less of an *ad hoc* nature. Daley, the professional, and Douglas, the amateur political leader, did not exactly hit it off at first. In 1951 Douglas was strong for General Eisenhower as the Democratic nominee; then, when it became apparent that the General's sympathies lay with the Republicans, Douglas was an eager supporter of Senator Estes Kefauver of Tennessee, whose organized-crime committee investigations had more than upset some segments of Chicago Democratic political life. Daley, who was close to Governor Adlai Stevenson, felt that Douglas' actions were those of a free-swinging bull in a political china shop; besides, he knew that powerful Democrats both locally and nationally were grooming Stevenson for the Democratic nomination.

When Daley became chairman of the Cook County Democratic Central Committee in 1954, he felt it would be a good idea to dump Douglas, who was up for re-election, and replace him with an old boyhood friend, William J. Lynch. Labor union leaders and some other powerful Democrats intervened, and Douglas stayed on the ticket. But, he admitted later, he had learned his lesson about trying to take a hand in party affairs. With this tacit understanding, that Daley would leave the Senate to Douglas if Douglas would leave the practical politics to Daley, the two men became closer than mere strange bedfellows. In the Eisenhower-Kefauver fiasco, the two men exchanged words which, while not forgotten, at least were ignored in the later years of Douglas' active political life. Douglas came, after Daley was elected Mayor in 1954, to have a grudging respect which grew to open admiration for Daley as a professional who could handle enormous problems in a professional way. For his part, Daley accepted Douglas as an able representative of the people of the state of Illinois and a winning politician in his own right—in a politician a characteristic that has never failed to impress the Mayor.

But, as with the majority of his Senate colleagues, Douglas' personal interests and Daley's are poles apart. Daley is the bootstrap Irishman from the Back of the Yards, the rough-and-ready political practitioner who believes in power—not for its own sake, but for what it can accomplish. Where Daley was a pragmatist, Douglas was a theorist, a scholar who could always find a classical allusion for what he was after. His high-ceilinged office in the Old Senate Office Building was, during his tenure, a mental decompression chamber for reporters who wanted the Douglas wit and language to lave them after a heavy day of what passes for oratory on Capitol Hill.

In his office hung portraits of two Renaissance scholars—one a gilt-framed oil of Erasmus, the other a sketch of Sir Thomas More. "Those two fellows are important to me," he told a visitor not long after his defeat. "They are a good brake, or a sort of warning signal, at least. You see, both of them were professors of sorts. One went into politics and lost his head. The other stayed out of politics and kept his. I find it very useful at times to ponder which was the smarter of the two."

Tom Littlewood of the Chicago *Sun-Times,* who watched Douglas for more than a decade both as an Illinois political writer and as a Washington correspondent, summed up his Senatorial role neatly during the last Douglas campaign:

> His function has been as a plodder, to plow the ground and pre-pare the way with ideas that often seemed kooky at the time, just as old-age pensions and unemployment compensation seemed far out in the '20s. His influence has been cerebral. He has not been a powerful leader like Lyndon Johnson, an effective manipulator of economic interests like the late Sen. Robert Kerr of Oklahoma, a technical specialist like Sen. Richard B. Russell of Georgia, or a showman like Sen. Everett M. Dirksen. Nonetheless, in 1950 President Harry S. Truman was compelled to veto Kerr's natural-gas bill because Douglas had succeeded, not in killing it, but in framing the issue in terms of consumer impact.

But by 1966 the character of politics had begun to change. For one thing, the Illinois voter was changing. The ethnic groups were shifting out of the center city and into the new housing develop-ments, becoming more conservative in their outlook as they did so. The struggle for civil rights, ironically, was leaving its pioneers like Douglas in the background and calling for a new broom wielded by a new breed to change the old ways, to clean out the Democratic organization in Chicago. The advent of the slickly packaged campaign, the push-button issues, the expanded use of television was making old-fashioned campaigns and old-fashioned campaigners obsolete. "Paul knew it would be tough," an associate said of him.

But for a half-century Douglas had spoken out on the issues, attacking and defending. Besides, the job was not yet done. He wanted to strengthen his truth-in-packaging bill, and to enact into law a similar "truth-in-lending" measure. It was a typical Douglas fight that was shaping up: in one corner, the Senator, who believed that the consumer should have spelled out for him exactly the amount of interest being charged him on an installment loan or an installment purchase; in the other corner, the banks, the automakers, the small-loan companies, all of whom quite naturally preferred to continue with the old system, where an announced rate of 6 percent, say, could cover a multitude of sins, through discounts, through fine print, through carrying charges, so that a 6 percent loan was actually a 12 or 18 percent loan.

To carry on that fight, however, it was first necessary to be re-elected. And Paul Douglas, whether on the picket line or the battle-field in the Senate, had never been a man to turn his back on a fight.

This was the kind of opponent whom Percy was taking on in his all-or-nothing contest for the U.S. Senate; if Douglas won, Percy's political sun would be in eclipse. And if Percy won, he would be able to start his Senate career with the reputation of a preliminary boy who managed to knock out the champion.

Through the spring and summer, Douglas was in Washington during the week, returning for weekend campaign appearances only. And Percy's campaign was starting slowly, with an eye to major speeches here and there, but with comparatively little activity.

This was being done on purpose. In July Houser told a Chicago reporter that the prime concern was with "tempo and build-up." The gubernatorial race two years before, he said, was "a seventeen-month campaign and there was a leveling-off period that came too early. We had no fast finish. This time, we're after a crescendo build-up. There's a more conscious holding back now in the summer." What Percy was trying to do, Houser said, was "to run a campaign which is responsive to what is on people's minds, and that means Vietnam and inflation. Being the challenger, you can't avoid the position of being critical, but we're trying to come up with positive statements and programs—education, housing, all the problems of urban living."

The voters Percy would be concentrating on were the independent and Democratic voters in Chicago, the Cook County suburbs and exurbs and those in the larger population centers downstate, such as Peoria and Rock Island. Downstate, too, there were union votes to be gone after, in places like Macon County, where the factories spring out of the cornfields, and the tractors plow and harrow right up to the cyclone fences around the industrial installations.

The Percy campaign had also taken a leaf out of Mayor Lindsay's notebook as well, and in Chicago staff aides planned to set up the neighborhood campaign centers that Lindsay and his campaign manager, Robert Price, had used so effectively in New York. Lindsay and Price even sent an expert from New York to help the Percy forces organize the headquarters. The basic trouble, however, was that there were never enough of them to be of any real help, they were not as well staffed as Lindsay's, and they sometimes were set up in competition with the regular Republican organizations. "They tried to copy one operation without adapting it to local problems," said a New York politician who gave some advice to Percy and Houser on the centers.

The real innovation, however, was Percy himself. In the two years since his uncomfortable performance in 1964, he had become more relaxed, and he was dealing with issues that he could feel enthusiastic about. With voters, too, he was more friendly, less the standoffish executive. He had developed some tricks to help him as well. For example, Percy in 1964 would often fall into the politician's hated trap of saying the same thing to the same voter twice on a walking tour or in a shopping center or a subway station. (A reporter who covered Lindsay's mayoral campaign remembered that Lindsay had once shaken hands with him three times in as many blocks on a walking tour in Brooklyn, much to the candidate's chagrin and the reporter's amusement.) To counteract this, Percy carefully pinned a button on everyone he talked to—on the chest for men, on the collar for women, and anywhere he could find when he was campaigning on Lake Michigan beaches. (Reporters and campaign aides on the beach tours watched with ill-disguised glee as Percy, trying to hide his discomfiture, looked over the available space on a bikini.)

"You know," said a downstate political writer to Percy after a day of campaigning in August, "two years ago the nickname Chuck didn't fit you. Now it does."

Percy was also working more closely in this campaign with the downstate chairmen, and it was having its effect. But he did not leave his campaigning completely in their hands. One summer night, he sat in the front seat of a car as it rolled along the highway. He was talking about a forthcoming tour of a downstate county with the chairman of that county. "During the day," Percy said, rhythmically slapping the back of the seat for emphasis, "I don't think I should even *see* a Republican. I should be out meeting Democrats. There'll be plenty of time at the rallies at night to see Republicans." He had learned a lot since 1964.

The pattern of the campaign, through the summer and into September, followed a standard pattern: a luncheon and/or dinner speech, shopping-center and factory-gate appearances, strategy meetings with aides and, where possible, a day a week out for studying the drafts and research for position papers. From January on, there had also been a series of day-long meetings, more seminars than skull sessions, with a visiting expert at each one discussing his area of competence—foreign policy, economics, civil rights.

It was going pretty much according to plan, and the polls were showing few unexpected weak spots. But then came September 18, a low moan from a bedroom, a mother's horrified scream, and the bottom dropped out of Percy's world.

CHAPTER *9*

Return of a Campaigner

The big room on the thirteenth floor of 100 West Monroe Street had been used for many things during the campaign—a place to sign up volunteers, to stuff envelopes, to drink Cokes and coffee and chat. Around the corner, down a corridor, was the office where Valerie Percy had worked, and on the morning of Wednesday, October 5, the big room was full of her.

The atmosphere was tense, almost strained. All the trappings of a major press conference were visible. The television and light cables snaked their way across the floor; the cameras were set up, their lenses trained, like the rifles of a firing squad, on a small table covered with green cloth and holding a battery of two dozen microphones. But the usual pregame banter was missing. Technicians and reporters worked quietly and chatted in rare quiet tones among themselves.

The unasked questions hung in the air: How would Percy comport himself? Could he get through this, his first appearance since Valerie's funeral, without his composure breaking? And, more important to the political writers, what hints would there be in his statement of the kind of race this new campaign had to be? Aides such as Houser had said that it would be more subdued, and common sense had added that there would be little of the street-touring and handshaking that had gone before; Percy would not want to subject himself to well-meant but heart-tearing expressions of sympathy from voters.

Shortly before eleven o'clock, the room began to fill with his staff, who had come to see the candidate, most of them for the first time since the funeral. The secretaries and volunteers lined the walls outside the cordon of cameras and reporters and waited, talking in the same hushed tones that had been used by the earlier arrivals.

A few minutes after the hour, a side door opened, and Chuck Percy took a dozen measured steps across the vinyl floor, and walked back into public life.

For eighteen days since the murder, he had been anticipating this moment. Now it was here—the time when he must tell the voters of Illinois what his plans were, how and when he would resume the race. Now he sat in the glaring pool of lights, turning his head slowly from side to side in response to quiet requests from photographers, nodding now and again at a familiar face among the reporters whose chairs crowded close to the table. Occasionally, he smiled tightly, but most of the time the jaw muscles worked slightly as if he were trying to steel himself against the next few minutes.

In slow and grave tones, he began to read the 231-word statement. The seventh word in the statement was "campaign," and it was the operative word. Chuck Percy was back in the ball game.

"Next Monday," he said, "I shall resume my campaign for the United States Senate. This is what I must do and what my family wants me to do. In order to spend as much time as possible with my family, my schedule will be less intense than before.

"But, with only five weeks remaining before the election, it is essential that the critical problems and great opportunities facing our people be thoughtfully explored.

"I shall continue to discuss the issues as clearly and forthrightly as I know how." Then he paused and took care of the question of a "sympathy vote."

"There can be only one issue in this campaign: Who will make the better Senator for the people of Illinois?" he said.

There were, however, indirect references to the murder. In an expansion of the statement which David Guyer had read to reporters in the driveway of "Windward" fifteen days before, Percy said that "on behalf of my wife, our children and myself, I want to say how deeply touched and grateful we are for the encouragement and concern expressed by so many in the past few weeks. Friends and those whom we have never met, members of my own party and members of the opposition, the press and law-enforcement officers have shown us a kindness and a consideration we shall never forget."

He thanked Paul Douglas, "who, at a difficult time for him, has acted generously, graciously and with understanding." Douglas campaign aides were to express privately a number of bitter reservations at the way their opposite numbers in the Percy camp handled the question of how and when to resume the race, but that was to come later.

Then Percy got to the meat of his statement. "This morning," he said, "I met briefly with my campaign staff and volunteers. My first public campaign appearance will be before the City Club at noon Monday."

He had finished. The ground rules were that he would answer no questions, and no one asked any. For a moment, he sat there. His eyes were set deeper in his head than many of those present had remembered them and the usually neat hair was down over the collar of his blue suit jacket.

He pushed back his chair, got up, turned and walked out, still with the same tight, slight smile on his face that had been there when he entered.

Beyond that, however, there was the clear indication that Percy was again in command, that he was a political man, and the inference was that the political side of him was the one he wished the voters to judge.

The statement had been nearly two weeks in the making. At first, after his arrival with his family in California, where the Percys had gone on the day following Valerie's funeral, the almost daily telephone conversations with Houser and other members of the staff had concerned themselves with personal matters, calls to be made to thank someone or to request errands to be run. Or they were calls to the Kenilworth police or the FBI to suggest something new that had just occurred to one or another member of the family which might be useful in the murder investigation. For example, Percy at one point remembered that the yard work for the Kenilworth house was handled by contract with a local service firm; the firm might be able to supply a list of workmen who had come to the house.

Each individual or family must find its own way back into the real world after a death, especially a death as hideous and shocking as was Valerie's. For the Percys, the road back was a typical family solution. For this family, which had spent so many hours playing together, the answer seemed to lie in strenuous physical exercise. For the first week, they went to a tennis camp in northern California, and for six, seven, eight hours each day played and played and played, working themselves into a state of physical exhaustion so that sleep could come without the drugs which their religion forbade them.

It was an emotion-charged time. During one match, Percy, who had been playing as hard as he was able, was suddenly overcome by his own grief and had to leave the court, in tears. Other family members were similarly hit at various times during the week. One presence which helped was that of Jay Rockefeller, Sharon's fiancé, who broke off his own campaign for the West Virginia legislature to be with his bride-to-be and her family. Rockefeller, with his grave, yet pleasant manner, was the perfect person, family members said later, to have with them at this time. He was someone who was involved with the family, his heart going out to it, but still not so closely tied that a slight change in expression, a chance word, would release the floods of emotion that the family was trying to learn again to control and to keep a private thing. The younger children were particularly taken with Rockefeller, and even the adults could weep in front of him without feeling that they were intruding on someone else.

There was prayer, too, and long walks, for those members of the family who wanted them, but more, there was quiet conversation. Much later, when family members could talk about the time, they talked about Percy's ability to bring God into discussions without making the implied suggestion that "Thy will be done" means a slavish acceptance of disaster as something that is all for the best.

Percy, too, was beginning to recover. He was reading again, he told Houser at one point, and had been deeply engrossed in a book on Vietnam. Slowly, he was beginning to think about other things.

Houser was ready as well. "When Chuck is ready to come back, we'll sit down and have a talk about it," he said during the early days of the family's seclusion. Now came the tougher part: just what sort of campaign would this new campaign be?

Calvin Fentress, a top aide, and Percy had both been working on a resumption statement for more than a week. They discussed it on the telephone, and then Fentress sat down and whacked out a draft, which he air-mailed to Percy in California. Percy also worked out a rough draft, but instead of being able to go over Fentress' version, the two crossed in the mail and it was too late to do anything about them until after Percy's return.

So, on Tuesday night, Houser, Fentress and Cohen went to Kenilworth after the family had had dinner. They sat in the library and drank coffee and talked quietly about the impersonal things— other campaign races in the state, the Percy campaign downstate, other staff members.

Finally, about 10 P.M., Percy said, "Well, let's get at this," and they turned to the job of getting the final words on paper. Percy already had made changes on Fentress' original draft, and the answer slowly evolved as to how to refer to the murder so that the reference could not possibly be construed by anyone as an attempt to enlist sympathy.

Words were suggested, debated, discarded. "Tragedy" was one which went through the mill. "Incident" was another. ("The incident" was the phrase Percy staffers had been using while the family was in California.)

After about two hours, it was decided not to refer to it at all, but to state, clearly and forcefully, at the outset that "there can be only one issue in this campaign."

That night in Kenilworth, Percy himself began to emerge from the protective shell which he had constructed for himself after Valerie's murder. The pattern of emergence had been slow to form, first on the telephone with Houser and Fentress and then later in the manner in which he volunteered to talk about the campaign, about his role in it, about how it should be conducted in the light of changed circumstances.

The possibility that Percy would withdraw from the race had never been seriously discussed by anyone, least of all by Percy himself. There was the question of the rest of the ticket and the commitment that others had made. But balancing this was the mental state that Loraine and the children were in.

Two thousand miles away, in a secret place, they were safe. What would it be like when they returned, walked up the driveway and climbed the stairs, looked at the door to Valerie's room? The nights were the worst, with Sharon and Loraine consumed often by what Percy later described as "jitters."

In addition, Valerie's murder was still an unsolved crime. "We have no idea who this—this nut was after," Percy said. "It might have been any member of the family or all members of the family for who knows what reason." So Percy, urged by Loraine, took a major decision. All campaigning would end shortly after nightfall; he would spend no night away from his family until the killer was caught. In addition, there would be heavier concentration on radio and television and on appearances before large audiences—luncheons, dinners, rallies. There were, at least for the time being, to be fewer face-to-face, man-to-man meetings with voters, partially because of the expressions of sympathy and partially because there was, purely and simply, a security problem.

The details of the new campaign were hammered out over the telephone, and the decision was made that Houser would call Victor Smith, chairman of the Illinois Republican State Committee, and break the news to the committee members at a meeting scheduled for the Conrad Hilton Hotel on Friday, September 30, just ten days after the Percys went into seclusion.

The word went out to Chicago's political reporters that Houser would have something of particular interest for the committee at the luncheon meeting, and when the announcement was made, Smith came out of the third-floor dining room to disclose that the campaign manager had "told us what we've been waiting to hear."

To reporters, Houser would give no other information other than the fact that Percy would return "early next week." The reason again was security. In conference with the detectives assigned to the case, it was decided that if the exact date were made public, the date would be changed. While there was speculation that the Percys would return Monday, the actual scheduled date was Tuesday, and Tuesday evening Percy, Loraine, Sharon, Mark and Gail arrived at O'Hare Field and were whisked by car to Kenilworth. Roger had returned directly to Menlo College.

In the meantime, the office at 100 West Monroe had begun to pick up steam. It had been officially closed since September 21, when a brief announcement by Houser suspended the campaign, but a skeleton staff had been kept on, to process the mail—now up to twenty thousand letters and telegrams—which had arrived after the murder. There were envelopes to be addressed to each person who had written; the mail had to be sorted and given priority; there was research that had been begun before the hiatus and which now had to be finished and put into the form of position papers and speeches.

The volunteer staff had been told on September 21 to go home and await word that the campaign would begin again, but somehow this did not seem to work. Little by little, people began drifting in again, settling down to their old jobs or pestering supervisors to be given something to do. Little by little, as that last week went by, the campaign office began to assume more and more the atmosphere of barely controlled chaos that should be the hallmark of a political campaign.

Instead of answering the telephones with "346-1600," as was done earlier in the mourning period, the switchboard operators, without direction, began again to say "Percy for Senator" to callers in those last few days.

Gretchen James, who had ably handled the scheduling of Percy appearances before the murder, now went to work again. Her task was formidable; great chunks of dates had gone out of the calendar, important dates in Chicago, in Cook County and downstate. Now the problem was to try to regain some of this lost ground, to squeeze two or three together for the maximum effect. The City Club, a bipartisan, good-government group, was a natural for a first appearance. A "Lawyers for Percy" luncheon a few days later was another good chance for maximum exposure; a student mock congress at Northwestern University in Evanston was put on the schedule.

This was the atmosphere to which he returned on Wednesday morning, October 5. He met with his staff, made his statement to the cameras and press, went back downstairs (where Cohen told him the inevitable had happened: a television camera had gone sour and he would have to read his statement again) and then held a few more brief meetings.

Then it was home to the big house beside the lake, where, for the next four days, he would help plan the campaign and, more important, use his icy self-discipline to help his family over the few worst days.

The resumed campaign started slowly, with the scheduled

speeches and the appearances formal and almost distant. But it began to gain momentum within a few days. Sharon came with Percy to one rally, and Loraine to another. Both were, for the first time since Valerie's death, publicly on view, and obviously nervous about campaigning. There was some private criticism of Percy for bringing them along, but who could say legitimately that this was not perhaps the best type of shock therapy to bring the family back into the campaign, to bring them outside of their private world of grief?

What it was all pointing toward was the big, four-day downstate campaign tour by train, a tour that had been arranged earlier in the campaign and which was designed to build it to a climax. Houser, who had some expertise, or at least a call on expertise, as a lawyer for the Burlington Route, had laid out the itinerary so that no Illinois voter who wanted to see and hear Percy would have to drive more than fifty miles to do so during the four days of the tour, which was to zigzag down the eastern part of the state, across the bottom, and then on up the west and across the north.

It was to be an old-fashioned barnstorming political swing, with a steam calliope (which never materialized), bands, posters and the gleaming train itself, on which would be stuck, in fluorescent tape, the legend "PERCY CAMPAIGN SPECIAL."

So, on October 27, with frost on the pumpkin and the fodder in the shock in downstate Illinois, the slick, savvy campaign hit its high, penultimate point.

Percy was vigorous as he pounded home his arguments from the observation platform in the little towns, chuckling now as he told jokes (with a repertoire that had built to three since the start of the campaign). He hammered away at inflation, at Vietnam, at government spending. And, quite suddenly, he found himself with a new, barn-burning issue. This was a promise to open, with Dirksen, a downstate Senatorial office, the first that Illinois had ever had. It touched a responsive chord with the downstaters, and downstate was where Percy had to get the votes to offset the expected huge Democratic turnout in Chicago. Another popular issue which drew loud applause here in this vestigial isolationist area was the question that he returned to consistently: "I wonder why we continue to give aid to and trade with those countries which trade with North Vietnam."

He did not carry the point further, or spell out how he planned to revamp the entire foreign-aid program to cut out the United Kingdom and France and other traditional allies, but each time he used it, more often in rural areas than in centers of population like Peoria or Rock Island, it struck an enthusiastic response. "It's not one of my favorite issues," said a campaign aide, listening to the crowd's response at one stop, "but they really seem to like it."

But the prospect of having another Senatorial office outside of Chicago was the point that seemed to invite the most attention. A Springfield reporter had an explanation as to why this hit so hard with the trackside crowds. "It's not so much that they feel cut off," he said. "It's just that Chicago to them is so superior-acting and, what the hell, they don't trust the city slickers, any of them."

But even that late in the campaign, it was the patronage-rich "pocketbook army" of Mayor Daley's Chicago administration that was the focus of much of the oratory, and Percy drew a picture of the Democratic faithful, turning out in enormous numbers on Election Day and "undoing all our efforts here." In addition to the bugbear of overconfidence, which Percy felt could change the public-opinion polls overnight, although the polls were showing him with a comfortable lead, this was a major point for the down-state swing, to stiffen the backbones of the county chairmen and the GOP regulars to greater efforts.

"What we generally did," said a campaign aide some months later, "was to bring the county chairmen aboard the train at the stop before their bailiwicks. They would go into the observation car and sit with Chuck and he would ask how it was going and they would talk with Chuck about the campaign until they got to the stop where everyone was going to know them and they'd listen to the speeches there and the cheers and applause and then, at the climax of the appearance, they would come out with Chuck onto the observation platform with everyone cheering his loudest. I tell you, there was hardly a one of them who wasn't almost peeing in his pants with pride when that door opened and he stepped out with the candidate."

And a few minutes after the train pulled away from the station, Percy would be handed the telephone by an aide and would talk to the local radio station for a "personal interview" to go along with the regular coverage. "We've had the most wonderful reception here. I'm so grateful," he would say, thereby assuring himself of a lagniappe to the already solid domination of the media he was receiving anyway.

There were a few scurries of unexpected activity as well, and in at least one of them Percy did not shine as the perfect candidate. Word reached him from Chicago, quoting an interview a few days earlier in the Chicago *Tribune,* in which he had purportedly said that he was against federal aid to parochial schools. In a small, impromptu press conference called for the Chicago reporters, Percy tried to get the *Tribune* reporter, an able and careful young lady named Donna Gill, to back off from her original version of the story, which she refused to do. He was petulant and managerial about it, and he also made the mistake of rebuking Miss Gill in front of other reporters, who seethed over the incident for several days after. The exchange is worth recalling only because it showed one of the rare, end-of-the-campaign cracks in his ice-cold control.

But as the train rolled through the autumn countryside, Percy became more and more relaxed, more often inclined, between stops, to walk with Loraine through the train and to chat with aides. It was very nearly impossible to believe that this was the man who had been so nervous and tense only three weeks earlier. He also talked about what he was going to do in the last ten days of the campaign.

"I think I ought to have more to say about foreign policy," he said, pushing a cup of rapidly cooling tea around the tablecloth in the dining room of his private car. "I think I ought to talk more about Africa, about the Middle East. We ought to be the mediator out there. Why let the Russians take the ball away from us?"

In his mayoral campaign in New York in 1965, John Lindsay had constantly harped, in speeches to volunteers, that with all the hard, slogging work that a good campaign entailed "there ought to be some fun, too. If it isn't fun, it isn't worth doing." On this trip, as the miles slid back down the gleaming tracks (some of which had not, to the riders' acute discomfort, been used by a passenger train in seventy-five years), the fun began to be more apparent as the reporters and staff members began to relax, cheered by the candidate's increased ease of manner, by the constantly rising percentages in the polls.

Percy himself was wryly amused at a tape recording, produced by a staffer, of a parody of the standard back-platform speech: "My opponent talks about the accomplishments that have come during his term in office. He is satisfied, he says. Well, I'm not a bit satisfied. I wish you could see the cracks in the deep end of the swimming pool at my house in Kenilworth, or the way the baseline is crooked on the tennis court. No, I'm not a bit satisfied. I'm not satisfied when my Mercedes Benz gets only twelve miles to the gallon or when Bell & Howell stock drops six points in the last year. And now I want to tell you a story about my wife Loraine. When Tiffany's opened its store in the Loop, Loraine went down to open a charge account, and she came back to me with the form and said, 'Charlie, what do I say here where it asks for husband's occupation?' I said, 'Loraine, you gotta tell the truth. Put down that I'm permanently unemployed.' Friends, on Election Day, with your help, we can make that dream a reality!"

The charge-account passage on the tape was a version of what came to be known as "the Mark story," which closed nearly all of the whistle-stop speeches. Percy's habit was to end his speech and, just before the train pulled out, to introduce his family— Loraine, Sharon, Gail and Mark—who would emerge in turn from the door of the observation car. Mark, the youngest, was invariably last. "I want to tell about my son, Mark," Percy would say. "A while back, Mark came home from school with a form which he had to fill out and it asked for 'father's occupation.' 'What do I put down, Dad?' he asked me. 'Mark,' I said, 'you've got to tell the truth. Put down "temporarily unemployed."' But, friends, with your help on Election Day, we can help Mark, so that he and I can go back to Joseph Sears School in Kenilworth and change that to read: 'Employed for the next six years for the good of the people of Illinois!'" Then the whistle would blow and the train would pull out, while the cheers rang out and the candidate waved.

At no time during the campaign was the age issue more apparent than on this glittering windup tour. It was in the young faces of Percy and his family, and in the campaign photograph— serious, with an open-necked white shirt—which were seen at every stop. It was more than implicit in some of Percy's remarks: "Age? All I know is that I'm forty-seven years old and I feel fine." "My opponent, who was also my professor of economics at the University of Chicago twenty-eight years ago . . ." "My opponent and his old-fashioned party of the thirties . . ." It was implicit, too, in the official campaign slogan: "A Strong New Voice for Illinois."

While Percy's campaign staff was slashing whole days of previous commitments from the candidate's schedule, Douglas and his aides were trying to double up dates, to make the days longer, to make up for lost time and lost ground from the three weeks the Senator had been idle. It was not a total success. Often, to the reporters who were covering him and even to members of his own staff, Douglas was a candidate with feet in clay, standard-bearer of a mired campaign.

The hurried rescheduling had meant that much of the earlier advance work had gone down the drain; on a downstate swing just after the resumption of the race, there were incidents when the motorcade got lost between one town and another, when the drum-beaters for a rally, sometimes alerted only hours ahead, were unable to attract more than a handful to the courthouse lawns in the little towns. At what had been labeled as a "fish fry" in one small town, ham sandwiches were served; the culinary import was small, but the political import indicative. The fish fry had, of course, been originally scheduled for a Friday.

If sometimes the campaign seemed inept, it was. But there was much more to it than that. The difference between the Percy campaign, by now shifting into high gear and moving along swiftly and efficiently, and the Douglas campaign, which punished the candidate with its long hours, its tiring, cramped automobile trips, lay in the basic approach of two candidates to two sets of voters. Douglas, as he had before, saw himself as "the People's Senator," and concentrated on meetings of precinct captains, or rallies, on handshaking in front of factory gates and in shopping centers. It was a shotgun approach, a person-to-person drive, leavened with at least one major speech a day, at a luncheon, a dinner or a rally.

In Chicago one day, Douglas scheduled a stop at Montgomery Ward's main mail-order house, and the intensity of his campaign came home to those who watched him lumber across the street, time after time, as the light changed and a new batch of workers left one of two buildings and headed like lemmings for the bus stops or parking lots. The Senator was determined to shake every hand he could. It was effective. But on another occasion, in a small downstate town, the schedule called for him to arrive at a factory gate at 4 P.M., and it was discovered later that whoever had been the local contact man had not bothered to check the factory's shift times; when Douglas arrived, only a few stragglers were leaving, since the shift had changed a half-hour before.

In the best organized Senate campaign this sort of thing will happen once or possibly twice, and the candidate vents his righteous annoyance on whatever aide was responsible, or possibly on whoever happens to be standing close by. When it happens more than once or twice, it is no longer annoying, it is heart-breaking. And it happened with hideous frequency in the closing weeks of the Douglas campaign, just when it hurt most. Douglas tried to make up for it with unscheduled stops. ("This looks like a likely corner, and we've got a few minutes; let's stop here," he would say.) Part of his regimen was a break each afternoon for a nap. As the race grew hotter and the days grew shorter and chillier, this went by the board as often as not in favor of a meeting with union leaders, with ward committeemen, with farmers who wanted the candidate's ear for a few minutes.

Part of this rescheduling was a compromise with the demands of the regular Democratic organization, particularly in Cook County. The Douglas staff felt that meetings at ward headquarters with precinct captains and workers were very close to superfluous, that if the organization wasn't on his side by then and ready to work for him, it never would be. In addition, the downstate campaigning in the closing weeks of the race was limited to a few day trips here and there, to places like East St. Louis, with its high proportion of Negro voters on whom Percy had been working hard. The concentration on Chicago then boiled down to an attempt to meet voters, shaking hands at factory gates, speechmaking and handshaking in shopping centers and on the street corners.

"We tried to go down the middle," said a top staff aide after the election. "What we ended up with was a formula under which we did what we felt we should do until about eight o'clock at night, and then we did what the organization wanted—hit the dinners and the ward meetings."

To offset the brutally punishing aspects of this schedule, a camping van fitted out with a daybed, a washroom and table, was hired. Douglas used this for relaxation between stops, to catch forty winks when he could, or even just to go in, draw the curtains and remove himself from public view for a few minutes. The Senator was cool to the very thought of using the van at first, but later became enthusiastic about its obvious advantages. He also became used to the idea of using a chartered airplane for his downstate whistle stops, something which he had not used to any wide extent in earlier campaigns.

For a man of seventy-four years, Douglas bore the strain of campaigning well, and indeed seemed to grow stronger as the politicking days grew longer and the times to rest shorter. There were some aspects, however, that were hidden from the voting public. Anyone who has been on a major campaign knows the strain it puts on the digestive tract: eating what one can when one can; the endless succession of "banquet" meals at political dinners which seem to have been planned by people who fear that chicken is about to disappear from the face of the earth; the growing horror with which one faces, as time goes by, the bottle of Coca-Cola or the cellophane packet of cheese crackers and peanut butter. Douglas had the added strain of being at the head of the ticket, the constant, gnawing knowledge that whatever he did or did not do would affect hundreds of people in the campaign. This is probably the worst burden a candidate has to bear, the feeling that if he has left undone those things which he ought to have done or done those things which he ought not to have done, he will be letting down all the others—professionals and volunteer amateurs who believe in him and his campaign.

As a result, the long hours, the grueling, stepped-up schedule took its toll in terms of weight, and somehow the weight seemed to come off the wrong places. He and his wife, Emily Taft Douglas, had decided at the outset of the race that he should lose some of his poundage—not that it was very great, but neither of them liked the idea of fat politicians. The trouble was that when he did lose, it came less from his middle than from his face. The lines showed deeper, the eyes seemed more staring. The signs, however, were illusory. Aside from minor stomach trouble, he was in good physical shape.

In "Countdown '68," a preview of the 1968 campaign, William Schecter noted that the "age issue" took other perverse forms.

Senators Robert and Edward Kennedy paid visits to Illinois to help Douglas, but "the Kennedy youth and vigor were stark contrasts to Douglas' age and immobility; he sat on campaign platforms, staring straight ahead, as if his mind was elsewhere, while others extolled his remarkable record."

As the campaign went along, age was becoming a sort of symbolic issue. Private polls taken by the Douglas camp showed that the question of age varied directly with other questions, particularly open housing. In some Cook County suburbs, for example, where traditionally Democratic voters were worried about the prospects of open occupancy, Douglas' age would be cited as a negative factor. It seemed to the Douglas camp that this was a sublimation of the open-housing issue, that people were too polite or too self-conscious to admit to a poll-taker that they were concerned with Douglas' stand for open housing, so they said they were opposed to him because of his age. "He's too old to be effective any more" could be translated, in the view of the Douglas staff, into "He wants me to have Negroes living on my block."

The age issue rankled with the Douglas forces, but there was little they could do to combat it. But more than that, they complained that they never seemed to be able to come to grips with Percy on issues, that "it's like trying to grab a handful of quicksilver," or trying to shoot at a target in a fog.

The whole Percy campaign had been built toward the final push, which was almost automatic, when the momentum had gathered such speed that it had a life of its own. But details were taken care of by tricks similar to those used in 1964, when members of the Percy family would try to get onto radio or television stations across the state. In Chicago, when Percy was campaigning in the evening, an aide would call various Chicago radio stations. When he finally got through to the news director or disk jockey, Percy would take over the telephone and the conversation would go something like this: "Hello, Pete [or Charlie or Bill]. This is Chuck Percy. I just thought perhaps you'd like to know what we've been up to tonight. We've been down here on the Southwest Side [or in Skokie or Des Plaines] talking to all these good people about the issues which we face in this campaign."

As quickly as one could say "unpaid political announcement," the tape recorder was hooked up at the station and listeners received the benefits of the candidate's thinking on "the issues which we face in this campaign" in the form of an exclusive interview.

And, although other things cost more—filmed commercials, posters, billboards, chartered aircraft and the train itself—that kind of operation only cost a dime.

The outward and visible signs of a typically modern political campaign, the first-cabin professionalism, were completely in evidence in the downstate tour; what was not in evidence was something that worried Percy, the possibility that an inward and invisible overconfidence might communicate itself to the voters, à la Thomas E. Dewey in 1948. There was the constant worry of what might happen when Mayor Daley's troops took to the streets on Election Day and what the volunteers in the Percy camp—a young, dedicated group, but amateurs for the most part—might find themselves faced with.

"I've been working with volunteers in this and a lot of other Republican campaigns," a GOP ward committeewoman said in Chicago in the last week of the race. "They're great, they really are. They work and work and work, right through the campaign. But they don't know, and no one can tell them; they have to see it for themselves: when that machine starts up and all the precinct workers are out early in the morning and late at night. These youngsters are fine; they've got all the right instincts, but they get so damned discouraged when they see the Democrats get moving. If they stick with it, though, they get tough, and that's what we need—toughness."

But in Chicago and its suburbs, the trend away from the Democrats and Douglas was already inexorable in this campaign. The Democratic party and the powerful unions, like the United Auto Workers and the Steelworkers, had put many of the blue-collar homeowners in the positions they occupied. Open occupancy, however, was frightening them, and they were pulling away. Precinct captains were being told by their workers that Douglas and his stand on open housing was too delicate a subject to talk about, and in some cases the campaign workers were learning to say, "Okay, I know how you feel; I'm a neighbor of yours. So if you want to vote for Percy go ahead. But this is the way you split your ticket so that the rest of the Democratic ticket can get in."

On Election Day Percy voted in Kenilworth and then, with Cook County Sheriff Richard B. Ogilvie, who was running as the Republican candidate for president of the Board of County Commissioners, toured polling places as part of "Operation Eagle Eye," a sharply conceived piece of campaigning which provided election judges and at the same time gave the impression that the Democrats would try to steal the election. None of the "Operation Eagle Eye" literature said specifically that the Daley organization was going to engage in widespread vote fraud, but the inference was clear.

In the evening Percy went to his private suite in the Sheraton-Chicago Hotel on Michigan Boulevard and waited for the returns to come in. It was almost anticlimactic. Downstairs, in the King Arthur and Camelot rooms of the hotel, the volunteer and other campaign workers and their friends were whooping it up in true Pepsi-generation style, the combo thumping out the beat for the wild dances.

Down the street a mile or so, the Douglas campaign workers watched with increasing gloom as Percy's lead lengthened. Finally, Douglas, with his wife at his side, entered the room to the thunder of cheers from those who had worked for him, many of them now in tears. He made his brief statement and then went home to bed, and thirty years of public service went with him.

In the Sheraton-Chicago, after he had received Douglas' concession statement, Percy came into the Camelot Room and mounted the small stage to make his own victory statement. He talked about carrying on in Paul Douglas' tradition and briefly mentioned Valerie. Then he, too, went home and went to bed.

As Percy climbed onto the stage, two reporters climbed onto a table for a better view. Behind them, a North Shore resident complained about his line of sight being blocked, and said that "we elected him, after all." One of the reporters, a Washington correspondent in Chicago for the election, turned suddenly and snapped: "It was hatred that elected this guy, and don't you ever forget it."

It was an emotional statement and only true in small part. Race hatred had played a role, but so had hard work and the issues of Vietnam and inflation and the fact that a younger man took on an opponent who was twenty-seven years his senior and who headed a campaign that never seemed to have the needed spark and flame in it. More important, the people of Illinois were speaking, at the polling booths, in the accents that other Americans were speaking in the fall of 1966—accents of a troubled, confused nation, torn by a social revolution at home and a war they did not understand abroad.

The verdict was in. The three-year road had been traveled to its end and Charles Percy had at last achieved the victory that he had sought for so long.

CHAPTER 10

The Issues:
Business, Right and Wrong

At the age of thirty-one, less than three years after he was elected president of Bell & Howell, Percy was asked to address the Economic Club of Chicago, an organization as august and high in aggregate income as its name might imply. His assigned topic at the dinner was "a management program for the future"—the future being the next quarter-century. He started the meeting with the showing of a five-minute segment of a film called *Deadline for Action*, produced by a left-leaning labor union. The film, needless to say, did not place American business in its best light; indeed, there was heavy emphasis on lockouts, strikebreaking and other low points in the long and tangled history of labor-management relations.

"When I first saw this film in its full, poisonous thirty-minute version," Percy told his audience after the lights had gone back on, "I was as sick at heart as I imagine you are now. Shall I make you feel even worse? Eight million Americans—tens of thousands of college students—have already seen and others are presently seeing these lies. An outstanding manufacturer told me about the bewilderment of his daughter after she had been shown this film in college. He said she actually had hatred in her eyes against American businessmen."

That evening in 1952, Percy first articulated before a large audience his ideas on business, its image and its future. He returned to them many times in the fifteen years that passed before he moved into national political prominence, but the words, spoken that night by the young, serious "boy wonder" of U.S. business, still represent his basic ideas on the role of management in the technocratic society.

"We are concerned," he said "about how far our technological advances have outstripped our human-relations progress in business. We are worried about the failure of management as a whole to recognize that business is a social as well as an economic activity. We are concerned about the too-frequent inability of labor and management to find a way in which they can work together toward a common objective. We are also concerned about management's relationship with the public and with government.

"We have good reason to worry."

As far as employees are concerned, he said, there are "certain basic desires that must be satisfied in addition to a pay check at the end of each week." First, there is the desire to be treated as an individual, and second, the desire to feel that as an individual an employee may express his opinion and have that opinion heard.

At Bell & Howell, Percy said, employee-opinion surveys had proved helpful. "We have asked our employees what they think of their boss, and, as a result of this particular survey, we established a 'college of supervisory leadership,' which is now attended by our supervisors as well as by potential supervisors. Before constructing our latest plant, we asked our employees' opinion as to features that they might want and color schemes and as a result introduced many desirable changes. We asked our employees about our company cafeteria, and as a result appointed an employee committee which is now managing it far better than we ever did before."

In a democracy, Percy said, the legislative process is itself an expression of opinion, and he wondered whether the same principle might not be applied in an industrial organization. At Bell & Howell, he said, it seemed to work. "We have been amazed at how fair and how sensible are the ground rules which our employees have made for themselves. There is no question about the fact that observance of them has been far higher."

Percy's amazement that people acting in concert will generally make reasonable decisions may have been a trifle ingenuous, but the program which he outlined for informing employees of corporate policies and actions was not. When he first came to the company, Percy said, he was assembling cameras as a summer trainee while attending the University of Chicago.

"One day a worker turned to me, holding a camera in his hand, and said, 'Look at this camera, Chuck. The customer pays a hundred dollars for it, and I've got it figured out that it only cost the company fifteen bucks to build. The rest is all profit. Pretty sweet for someone, I'd say.'"

Percy said that although this statement was of course untrue, "will you believe it when I tell you that for several years afterward I accepted it as a fact that the company was making an eighty-five-dollar profit on each camera? The company, unfortunately, did nothing to change or correct my ignorance. Sales, earnings, costs and other financial matters were kept as closely guarded by our comptroller as atomic-bomb secrets. Even within our accounting division the work was split up so that it was difficult for any one person to put together the cost of a single product. It was not until years later that I finally saw the cost figures on that camera. The company was making an 8 percent profit margin. I decided then that if I ever had the chance, I would frankly and openly talk about financial matters with the organization."

Percy outlined the new company policy of "Family Nights," which included entertainment and lectures for employees and their families, and said that profits were discussed, "not in a defensive way, but to show how good our profits were and how good it was to have reasonable profits." He said he often wondered "if it is not management's sensitiveness—our unwillingness to talk about profits and our unwillingness to put in the necessary time to explain their purpose and function in a free-enterprise system—that contributes so much to the public's lack of understanding of profits."

One answer to Percy's question might be that Bell & Howell has never been a union shop; liberal wage scales and fringe benefits have been credited with defeating a number of attempts by unions to organize the company. In companies with strong unions management is traditionally less inclined to take loud vocal pride in profits lest unions cut deeper into shareholders' dividends.

Family Nights at Bell & Howell have long been a phenomenon in the Chicago area, and particularly under Percy's leadership. One former employee recalled, too, that Percy, who as president was much given to writing congratulatory notes to people for their contributions to the corporate well-being, often used the Family Nights to hand out his congratulations in person.

"I remember the first time I went to one of the Family Nights," the employee, who later rose to a key executive spot, said. "I was standing there with my wife and two oldest kids and Chuck came by and stopped and said, 'That was a heck of a fine job you did with that project.' Boy, you can imagine what that did for my ego!"

But in his speech to the Economic Club, Percy was not content to talk only about Bell & Howell, but built toward a conclusion in which he discussed the relationship of business to government and the community. "The first responsibility of business to government is to obey the law," he said. "Business leaders have long talked against corruption in local politics, but have we really done much about it? And before we try to find the source of corruption in someone else's back yard, shouldn't we again look first in our own? We know, for instance, that small bribe-taking among members of a city's police force can often be the initial breakdown of morals in government. And yet, on the streets of America, who is the corrupter and who is the corrupted when a solid citizen offers a five-dollar bribe, after breaking a traffic law, to an underpaid police officer with four children at home?"

Business, Percy said, has "long championed decentralization of authority from Washington, and states' rights," and he quoted a Chicago alderman, Robert Merriam, later to become Eisenhower's appointments secretary, who had asked him, "Chuck, why does business talk against concentration in Washington and yet run there for many things which could be done at the local level?" Percy said he believed that "one of the most powerful single steps we could take in cleaning up national politics would be to attend more carefully to our local politics. As Adlai Stevenson [then Governor of Illinois] put it: 'The issue really is not that of states' rights, but rather state wrongs.'"

In the next quarter-century, Percy said, "management must assume a far more aggressive and challenging role in the economic, social and political life of our community and our country. Today it is the factors beyond our control that create many of our problems. The coming era is one that will present a tremendous challenge to American business management, but also a tremendous opportunity. The job we face is one of strengthening our society by placing as much emphasis on the development of moral and spiritual values as we have placed on technological progress in the past twenty-five years. It is a job on which management needs help. It is a job that requires the coordinated efforts of education, religion, government, agriculture, labor, finance, commerce and industry. Together, we must establish a basis for common understanding and common objectives. The public interest must be placed above selfish interest."

In that speech, Percy began, to all intents and purposes, his habit of using an anecdote to illustrate his point.

"One Sunday morning," he said, "a small boy went to his father and asked that he read the comics to him. The father, absorbed in a book, didn't want to be bothered. But the lad was persistent. Finally, the father cut up a map of the world into many pieces, like a jigsaw puzzle. And he promised his son a dollar if he could put the map together again. In fifteen minutes, the boy had finished and the father was astounded. Every piece and parcel had been put together to perfection. When his father asked him how he did it, the boy answered: 'Dad, on the other side of the map is a picture of a man. I put the man together, and you know, when I made the man right, the world was right.' "

This speech was delivered a dozen years before Percy sought his first elective office. The attitudes toward business and government did not change in the intervening years, but rather became sharper and more delineated. But something was stirring in that speech, at the beginning and at the end, that was to come to fuller flower as the years went by. That was his opening and closing references to young people—the college girl who hated businessmen because of a union-produced film she had seen and the little boy who made the man right so that the world would be right.

In May, 1967, at a black-tie dinner in Los Angeles inaugurating a new building devoted to business administration at the University of Southern California, Percy combined the two themes—business and youth—in remarks which brought home his concern with the image that business had created for itself—and with little help from union films—in the minds of youth. He noted that a recent poll had shown that only 20 percent of high school seniors showed any interest in entering business as a career. The nation, he said, was living in "confusing times," with a "revolution against social injustice at home and a prolonged war overseas." Young people, Percy said, were caught up in the toils of this confusion and were turning their backs on business. It was up to management, Percy said, to show that businessmen could "become a socially conscious community which can attract these young people into careers that blend commerce and public service."

But this was only part of it. Earlier in the day, at Berkeley, Percy had spoken on the steps of Sproul Hall at the University of California to an audience of three thousand students and faculty members. There he had talked to the students about their role in the world (and also flicked a glove neatly in the face of California Governor Ronald Reagan, archenemy of University of California students).

"There are those," he said, standing in the bright Pacific sunlight, "who would forever talk of 'the mess at Berkeley' perhaps because it is more reassuring than talking about the messes in Chicago, Watts or Washington." He cited the 901 Berkeley students in the Peace Corps and other service organizations and the students' "courageous commitment to the civil-rights movement long before it was fashionable."

Berkeley, he said, "is a symbol of protest to the world of your generation's mistrust of the American Establishment. Some of us do hear you and we do not dismiss the questions you raise. In the midst of war and injustice and poverty, our consciences cannot sleep. While we do not understand everything you say and do, we still share many of your concerns. We are increasingly sensitive to the fact that you can't measure the quality of American life by the number of color TV sets or nuclear warheads which we possess."

Young people, Percy said, had raised "stern questions about the basic values of our society's ruling institutions, institutions that have become so powerful that they have lost sight of their ultimate purpose." Among the offenders, he said, were "automakers who have had to be dragged in by their heels to adopt safety measures," newspaper unions "grown so powerful that they have helped to drive four New York newspapers out of business in four years," corporations guilty of price-fixing, utilities that "fight and ignore" measures aimed at reducing air and water pollution, "doctors who oppose

Medicare, and the National Rifle Association which opposes gun-control legislation."

Standing near the fringe of the crowd that May day were Percy's daughter, Sharon, and her husband, Jay Rockefeller. Sharon had worked the previous summer as a volunteer in "Crossroads Africa," a private organization which President Kennedy once called "the progenitor of the Peace Corps." She and her husband, who were married in April, had just returned from their wedding trip to the Far East, and were having a family reunion in San Francisco.

Seeing the Rockefellers there, one observer could not help recalling a remark Percy had made the summer before, sitting late at night on a hard bench outside an operations shack on a cow-pasture airport in a little downstate Illinois town. Percy was talking about a luncheon he had been given that day by a group of editors from a chain of small Illinois newspapers. The questions they had asked were tough, he said, and he recalled one in particular.

"They asked me whether I considered myself more an Eisenhower man than a Kennedy man, whether my views were closer to Eisenhower. You know what I told them? I said that for his particular time in history President Eisenhower was one of our greatest Chief Executives. But I told them, too, that he wasn't the one who got my daughter Sharon to go to Africa. Jack Kennedy did that."

Percy's years at Bell & Howell not only imbued him with a concern for youth, but taught him, too, that government can do only so much for business, and vice versa. In the area of foreign trade, Percy was at once in favor of keeping business free abroad —as in the area of East-West trade—and in favor of keeping government out of the business of being protective to special-interest groups. In the Senate, he differed sharply with Dirksen on the question of high tariffs. In October, 1967, before the Business Council meeting in Hot Springs, Virginia, Percy made his position clear.

"I, for one, do not intend to stand by while the interests of the public are abused in favor of some segments of American industry," he said. "I don't want to see the Senate serve the interests of a small group of industries while the man in the street foots the bill."

He also predicted that if protectionist legislation were passed, there would be retaliation by "foreign countries whose export sales to the United States are adversely affected." Such a retaliation, he warned, would mean a weakened dollar, a drain on gold supplies, an adverse impact on the balance of payments and loss of jobs in American industry. "In my own state of Illinois," Percy said, "one out of eight jobs depends on foreign trade."

The immediate battle, he said, was to defeat the protectionists who sought higher tariffs. "We must turn our attention to the true fiscal causes of the current protectionist campaign. Imports cannot be an excuse for failing to confront the underlying economic problems before us."

By the magnitude of its economic strength, Percy said, the United States "dominates free-world affairs. We have attempted to use this responsibility for leadership wisely, through multilateral action among all free world nations. . . . It was mutilateral action which recently resulted in the greatest international trade negotiation ever consummated—the Kennedy Round. In the fields of disarmament, balance-of-payments adjustment, international monetary policy and less visible but equally important areas, the United States exercises its leadership in a community of nations. After thirty-five years of progress, to regress to unilateral action would be an admission of defeat by American business. I can't believe that the business community in which I have lived and worked for over a quarter of a century is willing to make such an admission."

A few days later, on October 26, Percy took his fight against protectionism to the floor of the Senate.

"At a time of economic upturn, it is surprising that we find a whole range of industries seeking special measures designed to interrupt the normal operation of the marketplace and create special economic terms for some industries at the expense of others, not to mention the consumer or the national interest," he said. And he pointed out that "almost 90 percent of the members of this body, and an equally large proportion in the House, have introduced bills proposing import controls, mainly quotas."

Percy described the quota system of controlling imports as "a particularly insidious form of trade protection. It is, in effect, a thinly disguised subsidy, the cost of which is impossible to calculate."

And he returned to his business background to hammer home his theme. "As a former industrialist who has faced the sometimes crushing problems of stiff import competition from Japan and Germany particularly, my associates and I also faced the question: should we ask for protection from foreign competition or fight for our markets, here *and* abroad? We answered that question and chose the marketplace."

While Percy retained some skepticism about the total dedication of both politicians and businessmen to the ultimate goals of the Republic, he still preferred—probably naturally—the company and advice of his fellows in industry and commerce. This attitude created considerable political trouble for him in late 1967 and early 1968, when he gave his blessing to "The Percy Group," an organization of Chicago businessmen which sought to relieve him of some of the financial burdens of running his three Senatorial offices—in Washington, Chicago and Centralia, where he shared expenses in a downstate office with Senator Dirksen.

"The Percy Group" sought, chiefly using the lists of heavy campaign contributors, to extract pledges of $500 a year from two hundred leading Chicagoans, to put those funds into a tightly-managed, completely audited fund which would pay some salaries, buy some equipment and in general replace the $75,000 a year it was costing Percy out of his own pocket.

The aim of the fund may have been acceptable or not, but in the political and public-relations sense, it was a fiasco. Its formation was never announced publicly; indeed, the St. Louis *Post-Dispatch* first disclosed its existence in a blaze of unfavorable publicity. Then, a short time later, the Chicago *Sun-Times* found out that there was no intention of making the names of contributors public and launched a campaign, via news stories and editorials, to bring the names into the open.

The first reaction by the organizers was to say that a contribution to a United States Senator was the same as a contribution to the Community Fund, that it certainly could be done anonymously. Later, however, this was modified, particularly when Percy said on "Meet the Press" that he had no objection to public disclosure of the names, provided those who had already contributed or pledged were given a chance to withdraw from the fund if they obected to having their names made public. In January, the solicitation of funds was dropped on Percy's orders and the money returned.

The incident left a sour taste in a number of mouths, particularly in Chicago, where the fund was viewed, in the words of one observer, as a "public-be-damned try by a bunch of Chicago Club fatcats to keep a piece of the Percy action."

Whether it would do any long-range political harm would not, of course, be known for some time. But it stained the Percy image of the "problem-solver"—something he had been at pains to build.

As the decade of the 1960s began to grow into middle age, there emerged on the face of American politics the "problem-solver," the man of government or business or both who had proved himself, one way or another, not by painfully climbing a political ladder from precinct to Congress or State House, but reaching his goal by a different route.

America, it became clear in 1966, was beginning to tire of old lines of authority. Union leaders could no longer deliver their membership to one candidate or another and sometimes could not even deliver their membership once they had negotiated a successful contract. To big-labor negotiations, a new ingredient was added: whether the membership of the local would ratify the contract once agreement had been reached by negotiators.

In politics, the individual candidate became more important than the party, in many areas. In New York, John Lindsay in 1965 campaigned as a Republican on the theme that New York City could be governed and defeated a tired, fatalistic Democratic organization. Earlier, John Kennedy had put together his own organization and had seized the nomination and won election on the basis of "It's time to get this country moving again." Lindsay later echoed his thought, so did Percy with a recurring theme, counterpointed with references to "the tired old slogans of the New Deal," whose basis was dissatisfaction with the status quo.

In 1966 it was Ronald Reagan's turn in California. Just as in New York City, the voters of California were fed up with the same, bone-weary clichés and spit-and-baling-wire patchings of the Democratic administration of Governor Edmund G. (Pat) Brown. In New York Governor Nelson Rockefeller won a smashing reelection victory on the platform of accomplishment in eight previous years.

Many things differentiate all the above-named political figures. But they have one thing in common. Their approach to the voters was that of the problem-solver—not the Republican problem-solver or the Democratic problem-solver, but the individual problem-solver. During the 1965 New York mayoral election, Lindsay effectively quoted his patron saint, Mayor Fiorello La Guardia, who said once that there was no Democratic way to clean streets and no Republican way to clean streets; there were simply good and bad ways to clean streets.

But something more was happening as well, as the problem-solvers began to push to the fore. There was in the air a basic change in thinking among the centrists of both parties, a new look at partnership between business and government. In New Deal days, the business community had been labeled "economic royalists," and the university professors had been summoned to the battle, often with dubious results.

In the 1950s, President Eisenhower's millionaire-heavy Cabinet carried out probusiness policies which denied the GOP control of Congress for all but the first two years of the administration. And in 1962 President Kennedy, who was inclined to place his trust in politicians above and beyond their fellow mortals, lashed out in anger at the steel industry, when he felt he had been double-crossed on a price rollback, citing his father's warning that businessmen were all "S.O.B.s."

President Kennedy's younger brother, Robert, however, was one of those who felt the new synthesis. He roped business into slum-development projects in New York City's Bedford-Stuyvesant ghetto. Lindsay persuaded business to join in city projects. Rockefeller welded together business and government in a dozen projects across the state, calling on his political muscle and wide acquaintanceship in the private sector.

So it was with Percy, at least up to a point. The New Illinois Committee had been an attempt to put through, by the sole support of the private sector, projects which had previously been governmental. But the role of NICOM was more negative than positive. It was a gadfly operation in most cases, forcing the political power structure to take steps it was reluctant to take, such as in rat and insect control and in providing heat and garbage disposal.

But with the forging of the program for private ownership of low-income housing, Percy himself had begun to arrive at a new philosophy, one in which government was the innovator and the private sector was the operative force.

CHAPTER *11*

The Issues:
Ghetto and Suburb

Throughout the 1966 campaign both Percy and Douglas had searched for a way to handle the issue of open occupancy, but for Douglas particularly it was an enormously difficult question. Many of the Senator's staff aides, along with others working for the election or re-election of Democratic candidates, were annoyed or dismayed or both by President Johnson's decision in the spring of 1966 to press for federal open-housing legislation.

They did not doubt the legitimacy of the need, but many of them felt that the hope of passage was so slim that those candidates who were running for re-election would be recorded on a vote which would, in the immediate future, be futile and politically harmful.

It was an issue of pressure and counterpressure. For his part, the President was already feeling the beginnings of heavy pressure to bring the Vietnam war to some sort of solution; the "hawks" were urging stepped-up military measures, while the "doves" were claiming that the country was moving farther and farther into a bloody Asian sump, from which there could be no retreat, no escape.

Civil-rights leaders in the various urban communities were beginning to compare the national Democratic administration's commitment in Vietnam to its commitment at home in the field of civil rights. They predicted that a "long, hot summer" was approaching, and the administration felt it had to get on the record with some

116

sort of strong civil-rights measure, something to carry the provisions of the 1964 Civil Rights Act a long stride forward. The 1964 Act had established the principle of open housing, but it had concerned itself primarily with rental. In cities like Chicago the thrust of the Negroes was toward the suburbs, toward neighborhoods where better schooling was available more than toward areas marked by green grass and trees. This was the heart of the matter. On the Northwest and Southwest sides, two-flat apartments and bungalow houses were available, but real-estate brokers would not show them to Negro families. In cities like Chicago, too, the advance of equal job opportunities meant that thousands of Negroes were financially equipped to break out of the ghettos; a schoolteacher or a civil servant or a Transit Authority bus driver could afford to buy a house with a price tag of $18,000 or $20,000 or $22,000.

But the available housing was all in neighborhoods—at least in Chicago—inhabited by the very people who had fled the areas of earlier Negro encroachment; on the West Side, where the gray gimcrack six-flat apartment houses are called "Polish battleships" and the onion domes of the churches betray the proud immigrants' homesickness for the familiar in an alien land; on the South Side, where the ethnic strain is less pronounced, but where the absentee landlords have cut up the handsome old semidetached houses and red-brick apartment buildings, turning them into twentieth-century Black Holes of Calcutta whose prisoners are blamed for not maintaining suburban mores and morals.

Illinois had no statute on open housing, and in 1967, despite great efforts, attempts to pass a bill failed in the legislature. There was a city ordinance in Chicago which forbade discrimination in housing, but there was no real way to enforce it. The Chicago Real Estate Board, which might have taken the lead in pushing open occupancy as a moral question, called for the ewer and basin and said its position only reflected what people wanted.

In addition, Douglas was saddled with the Presidential desire to push for a federal open-housing statute. At Rockford, a town ninety miles from Chicago, staff members one day raised the issue with the Senator, suggesting alternative positions for him to adopt which might not be so politically dangerous.

Sitting beside a motel swimming pool, Douglas listened to all the arguments, nodding as the staffers made their points, occasionally asking a question. Then he thought for a minute.

"No," he said. "No. I've been for open housing for thirty years. I couldn't change my position now, even if I wanted to."

There, beside a motel swimming pool, a fateful decision was taken on a matter of principle. It was to come back to haunt him through the months ahead, and he would try his best to explain his stand to audiences both hostile and friendly. "There are many reasons why a man might not be able to buy a house," Douglas would say, sawing the air with his forefinger. "His credit might be bad. He might not be able to afford it. But no one should be able to deny a person the right to buy a house solely because of the color of his skin."

In contrast to this was Percy's stand on open housing. Douglas hit Percy for "vacillation" on the issue, charging that he had switched his position since the 1964 gubernatorial campaign. This was true, and it stung Percy.

In 1964 Percy had repeatedly stated that open-housing legislation was undesirable, that while he felt Negroes should be permitted to buy houses wherever they could afford to buy them, legislation was not the answer. Instead, he said, he urged the voluntary cooperation of real-estate brokers in showing properties to Negroes. But the realtors had no intention of cooperating. In the Chicago neighborhoods and suburbs where Negroes wanted to move, most brokers operate on a relatively small margin of profit; the competition is severe. The broker who voluntarily showed a listing to a Negro family would, in his own view, be a very brave man indeed. So it was easier for the brokers to say that they were there to serve the public and that the public didn't want houses shown to Negroes.

Percy, faced with this issue and with Douglas' taunts in 1966, had to make a decision. He had labored long and hard to build up a following among Negroes on the South and West sides and did not want to see this dissipated.

A campaign brochure prepared especially for Negro voters cited Percy's pro-open-housing position, and it was with this that Douglas started hitting him in October, charging that he had changed his mind, that he had once favored no legislation but now favored it. The Douglas camp also managed to see that the Percy brochure prepared for Negro voters was circulated in backlash neighborhoods.

Percy was in a political bind. He certainly had no intention of repudiating the pamphlet prepared for Negro voters. But if he came out too strongly for open housing, he would alienate the "ethnic" votes on the Northwest and Southwest sides of Chicago and in the suburbs. These were people who had been profoundly disturbed by the Negro marches, often accompanied by white counterdemonstrations, into their neighborhoods. The residents were traditionally Democratic, but began to show a number of soft spots now that Mayor Daley had come out in favor of open housing as part of a "racial summit" agreement in September, which had halted the marches. The whites felt the city Democratic administration had "sold out" to Martin Luther King and the civil-rights leaders. Archbishop (later Cardinal) John Patrick Cody of Chicago, the church leader who had integrated New Orleans' parochial schools, had sided with Daley and Dr. King, but not even this influence was having a great effect on the feelings in the all-white neighborhoods. The marches had come close to polarizing the city; slogans began appearing as graffiti on subway walls: "Cody doesn't speak for Chicago Catholics. They speak for themselves."

Percy took a compromise position. After a particularly bitter Douglas attack, he spelled it out: he was in favor of "the principle of freedom of residence," he told reporters. But, he said, he felt that the only possible law that could be passed and enforced would be one which excluded residential buildings with five or fewer dwelling units. It was the "Mrs. Murphy's boardinghouse" approach, and in the context of Chicago's tense and violent racial summer, still fresh in the voters' memories, it was a good one. To most Negro voters, Percy was reaffirming his stand on fair-housing laws; to the whites, the stand was not particularly distasteful since, in general, it did not affect them. The marches in the summer—in Belmont-Cragin, Gage Park, Marquette Park, and at Bogan High School—had all concentrated on neighborhoods where housing consisted, for the most part, of one- and two-family homes. Under the Percy formula, these should remain intact.

Politically, it was a good middle-ground stance for Percy to take. Douglas could not hit him too hard on the issue, except to say that "my opponent only wants fair housing in large apartment houses." The Senator probably did do himself some good with

Negro voters, however, through a poster with the legend: "You Know Where He Stands on Civil Rights!" But in the lower-middle-income white neighborhoods of Chicago and Cook County, resistance more than offset the gains in the Negro wards. Among the blue-collar whites, the tradition of unionism was strong, and in earlier elections the union troops had turned out for Douglas, ringing doorbells, supplying volunteers, money, halls, rallies. In the fall of 1966, though, many of Douglas' closest aides felt that the whole backlash issue was coming home to roost.

The big "vertical" unions, such as the Steelworkers and the Auto Workers, had been strong supporters of the civil-rights movement from its earliest days. But in Chicago this support did not extend to having Negroes move in next door. And the "horizontal" unions —the building trades in particular—while paying lip service to civil rights, had maintained their own discrimination. In their support of political candidates, they were not likely to work very hard for someone like Douglas, who was, as they saw it, trying "to reduce property values" by urging integrated housing.

Much was made after the campaign of Percy's "courting" of the white backlash. The fact was that he didn't seek the backlash vote. He had, in the years between the gubernatorial campaign and the Senate campaign, spent too much time and effort trying to cut into the Negro Democratic vote to risk throwing it away by making a racist appeal. He had, for example, encouraged and supported the "New Breed" on the South Side, which began to make its appearance in the spring of 1966 as a sometimes amorphous, sometimes crusading, sometimes amateur, sometimes professional group of young, tough-minded Negroes who owed no allegiance to Percy, no allegiance to Douglas, and certainly no allegiance to Mayor Daley.

To understand the New Breed, it is necessary to understand the South Side of Chicago, since it is an area which is in ferment, and, more particularly, an area in which the Daley method of governing a city is most apparent.

Southward from Cermak Road near Lake Michigan, the First Illinois Congressional District marches for eight and a half miles, seemingly breasting the northering Negro tide which formed it, swells it, lives in it. Southward it marches, through jammed and littered streets, past the public-housing projects thrusting their stark brick and steel and concrete functionalism high into the sky, a Dantean circle of hell in concrete pillars, devoid of aesthetic values, devoid of humaneness, devoid of hope. Southward it marches, now past Hyde Park High School, which has echoed to the alien sound of gunfire and which is often caught in the open war between the authorities and the powerful Negro youth gangs.

Now, as it moves south, the eastern boundary moves westward, to cut out the carefully and selectively integrated area around the University of Chicago. Then the slums begin again, and the boundary moves to embrace them, but in its southward move the six-flat and three-flat tenements lining the filthy streets give way to one- and two-family homes with neat lawns and clipped hedges.

More than 90 percent of the 400,000 people who live in the district are Negro, and if they were, some night, to disappear from the face of the earth, it would mean that one out of three Negroes in the state of Illinois would disappear.

The South Side is, in reality, two communities. On the north, ending at about Sixty-seventh Street, is the noisy, noisome ghetto of teeming streets, dilapidated housing, and the tall projects, with their asphalt playgrounds resembling prison exercise yards, their fixed park benches resembling prison furniture. South of Sixty-seventh, the neighborhood begins to change, the chain-mesh fences around the patches of mud and dust that pass for lawns begin to disappear, and smaller buildings become the rule rather than the exception. By the time the district bottoms out at Ninety-ninth Street, the South Side—synonymous outside Chicago with slums—has become integrated suburbia.

Economically, the enemy is a drainage economy: all but a handful of businesses are owned by whites, who take in money earned by Negroes outside the area and in turn remove the money to other parts of the Chicago area. Sociologically, the enemy is also typical of the enemy in any large city slum: in the poorer areas, the apathy born of the struggle for survival, the despair arising out of the fearful knowledge that today is like yesterday and that all the tomorrows are going to be like today; in the better neighborhoods, the apathy arising from run-of-the-mill bourgeois worries about jobs and mortgage payments and car payments and maybe sending the children to college.

So far, a fairly typical picture. It could be Watts or Harlem or

Bedford-Stuyvesant or Hough or the Central Ward in Newark. But there is a political complexion to the South Side which is different from that of other cities. For nearly twelve years of Mayor Daley's administration, the South Side was ruled like other sections of the city—through ward committeemen, precinct captains and precinct workers. There was the same system of rewards and punishments for political activity. A good worker became a captain, and with his captaincy he was given a steady job with the city or with the Cook County administration. The jobs weren't much—riding a garbage truck with the Department of Streets and Sanitation or a menial position at Cook County Hospital, for example—but they were better than what most Negroes in the ghetto had. Because no one could see an end to the Democratic rule of Chicago and Cook County, the security in pension plans and insurance schemes looked good, so the vote was turned out, year after year, election after election.

Monarch of all—or nearly all—he surveyed on the South Side was Representative William L. (The Man) Dawson, who in 1966 was making his eleventh bid for re-election to Congress. He was *primus inter pares*—the other Democratic ward committeemen—but still undisputed *primus*. He was in nearly complete charge of city, state and federal patronage among Negroes, doling the jobs out to ward committeemen and blessed with the power of veto.

But in 1966 things began to change. Dawson found himself seriously challenged. Seriously, that is, in the sense that if the threat was not serious, the challengers were.

Calling themselves the "New Breed," they were young Negroes who were college-educated (largely by way of basketball scholarships) and restless (largely by way of the armed services and particularly by way of Vietnam). They wanted no jobs as garbage-can heavers or bedpan jockeys. They had a goal, pure and simple, and it was to change the ghetto by making the Democratic administration compete for votes there. They had no alliances with the regular civil-rights organizations and none with any party. But, more important, they had no illusions about how tough their job was going to be. Their leader was David R. Reed, a giant of a man at six feet, four inches, a college graduate with no profession but politics and a veteran of Vietnam. Reed surrounded himself with other men of the same stripe and often size (the basketball scholarships again playing their part) and went to work in the spring.

Percy and Richard Ogilvie, running for County Board President, tied themselves to the New Breed, gave them some money, the opportunity to raise more in the lily-white GOP strongholds on the Near North Side and North Shore, and some instruction in the techniques of turning out the vote and putting a message across. Some of the instruction Reed and his cohorts needed, but they did not need to be told about most of the pitfalls. The South Side had for years had the reputation of a happy hunting ground for vote-stealing; it was here that enthusiastic deputies of Mayor Daley gave John Kennedy in some precincts almost more votes than there were voters. The New Breed also knew better than to split its forces in primary battles. For example, Fred D. Hubbard, a thirty-seven-year-old YMCA field worker, wanted to challenge Dawson in the Democratic primary. So did Reed, but he withdrew to keep the vote from being split. When Dawson smashed Hubbard by a six-to-one majority, Reed was ready to oppose him in the general election.

The New Breed's headquarters, in the heart of the South Side, was not a Percy headquarters—the Percy store front was four blocks away. But Percy's picture and Percy's literature were to be found around the various Reed store fronts throughout the district. And there was Percy money in the Reed headquarters. That, on the surface, was almost the extent of the alignment between the two candidates throughout the general-election campaign.

Percy and his campaign staff were wise enough to see that by standing more or less three paces to the rear of the leaders of the New Breed, they would help Reed in his drive to pick up independent votes and not weight him down with a borrowed Republican shield.

To paraphrase a famous statement, if Dave Reed had not existed, it would have been necessary for Percy to invent him. He needed some device, some end of the wedge, with which to push himself into the South Side. There was beginning to be political ferment there, and Percy, as far as most Negro voters were concerned, was a nonperson. They didn't know him. He had all but ignored them during the 1964 campaign, which was fought according to basically old-line Republican strategy, which meant writing off Negro votes for the most part.

After his defeat, he excused this refusal to go after the Negro vote by saying there were very few Republican Negroes anyway. In addition, if the gubernatorial campaign had brought out anything, it was that Percy was painfully shy among blacks. "He looks on Negroes as a concept," said one white South Side Democratic political leader. "He doesn't seem to see them as people with individual problems." Or, more to the point, his experience with Negroes had been about what could be expected of someone with his background. In the summer of 1966 one of Percy's friends, a North Shore housewife, was asked by a reporter whether she felt Percy's attitude toward Negroes had loosened in the two years between campaigns, whether instead of being shy and diffident around them, he had come to accept them more readily as individuals.

"Oh, no," was the reply, "Chuck has always been very much at home with Negroes. The family's had colored help for years."

Nevertheless, despite this relatively typical suburban approach, it was Percy who took the lead at Bell & Howell in opening the job ranks to Negroes in 1950, a year after he had taken over as president.

The conditions there had not been exactly rosy. Percy himself said later that the wartime experience at Bell & Howell, where Negroes were hired as night custodial help, had served to harden attitudes among the second-generation German toolmakers who made up the foremen and much of the skilled help in the workshops. "There were some troublemakers," Percy said, "and there was a knifing one night, and many people at Bell & Howell were judging the whole race on that one knifing incident." He had, he said, "always had the feeling that business management had to be ahead of the trend"—and the trend, he felt, was toward equal opportunities for Negroes.

In 1949, when he became president, the country was in the middle of a recession, and his attempts to hire Negroes were blocked by the presence of a long preferential rehiring list of workers who had been laid off earlier. In 1950, however, when the company had some room for new jobs, Percy tried to find out why it was that Negroes were not being taken on as apprentices or in other jobs. There was no union difficulty, since Bell & Howell had never been a union shop.

"When I started asking questions, I got all the answers you might expect," Percy said. "I heard that Negroes were stupid and shiftless and lazy, that if we hired them, we would have to have separate cafeteria and toilet facilities. So I contacted the Urban League and the National Association for the Advancement of Colored People and told them: 'You educate me; what arguments and counterarguments can I use against all these ideas I've had thrown at me here?' They got all excited. They wanted to put on a presentation for the foremen and personnel people and executives, but I said, no, I would take the rap."

The company put together a film showing how equal employment had worked in other industries and "summing up all the arguments in favor of hiring Negroes," as Percy put it. A short time later, he called together the plant's key personnel, ran the film for them and then said: "Those are all the arguments. Can anyone think of counterarguments? If not, I'm reporting to the board of directors that, beginning tomorrow morning, we start hiring regardless of race, color or creed." He added that if any of his listeners felt they could not live with the new edict, "you are free to leave now with honor," but the message was strong that there would be no job discrimination at Bell & Howell in the future.

An associate remembered that when Percy walked off the platform, "the sweat was running down his face, and he wanted to know how he had done." A short time later, the first Negro—a young technician—came into the skilled ranks at Bell & Howell.

Now Percy was seized with the zeal of the convert. In the Midwest, he said later, Bell & Howell was "years ahead of other companies. I used to go around to other companies, arguing with their executives. It seemed abhorrent to me that business, with its monopoly on employment, should restrict people because of race." Most of his arguments, however, proved fruitless, particularly with the companies where the large industrial unions did not have a strong foothold. "I finally decided you just have to do it by law," Percy said later. "You need the moral protection of the law to get anywhere."

Even some of Percy's toughest critics concede that he was among the first of the Republicans in Illinois to press for a fair-employment-practices law with teeth in it. But there is disagreement over how much he really helped the cause later in the game. For one thing, his critics say he caved in under pressure from fellow Republicans and fellow businessmen at a hearing in Springfield in 1962, when the appointment of Charles Gray, a former close associate at Bell & Howell, was up before the State Senate. Percy came to Springfield ready to testify in Gray's behalf on his appointment as chairman of the FEPC, but other Republicans, notably Senator W. Russell Arrington of Evanston, a man with a penchant for riding roughshod over his opposition wherever it comes from, did not wish further discussion.

In the hearing room, Percy passed a note to Arrington, asking that he be called. Arrington read the note, looked at Percy and slowly wagged his head from side to side. Percy later read his statement to reporters in the corridor, but those who were backing Gray felt that Percy had not done all that he could have. Percy claimed later that "Russ Arrington had originally told me that the committee would call me as a witness. Then as the hearing went on, they just simply didn't call me. They would not permit me to testify."

In answer to suggestions from critics that the hearing was public and that he could have pressed his demand to testify, Percy said the meeting was adjourned before he had a chance to renew his request.

A great deal of bitterness hung on after the incident, particularly among liberal Democrats who believed that Percy was something new in Republican circles in Illinois. They blamed pressure from businessmen and Republicans such as Robert Galvin, president of Motorola, whose company was a prime target of civil-rights leaders over discriminatory hiring.

Percy's involvement with and understanding of Negroes had not been easy to forge. There had been old, suburban attitudes to overcome, a cavalier disregard, in the name of political expediency, of their plight and potential. But out of the turmoil in Percy's mind came the seeds of his major domestic program—private ownership of housing for low-income families.

CHAPTER 12

The Issues:
Housing—The Idea

Freshman Senators and Congressmen, when they first come to Washington, are all too frequently inclined to do one of two things —either burst full-blown on the scene like self-styled reincarnations of Daniel Webster or George Norris or Sam Rayburn with a hatful of bills (largely of the special-interest variety), or stand around with their hands in their pockets waiting to be told what to do by their elders and betters. Despite a couple of initial miscues, Percy did neither when he set up shop in ex-Senator Maurine Neuberger's offices in the Old Senate Office Building.

What Percy had going for him from the outset was a pet project which was tailor-made for the kind of image he and his close Senate Republican associates wanted him to project. The image was, in part, that of the problem-solving urbanist, the "can-do man," the lawmaker with all the qualities of what former Harvard president James Bryant Conant once described as the "tough-minded idealist."

The project, the hook on which Percy could hang his domestic image, was the National Home Ownership Foundation bill, which, if it could be enacted, would help low-income families to own their own homes, thereby—at least this was a major aim of the proposal —instilling in them a sense of pride in their own property. It was to be Percy's first major piece of domestic legislation and was not only to keep him well occupied but also to serve as an excellent survey course in the legislative process. In December, 1965, when Percy decided to run, he had been asked by Everett Dirksen, perhaps somewhat patronizingly, whether he was willing to learn the law-making process; NHOF would give him an excellent chance.

The idea had not sprung full-blown from his brow; in fact, it was not, originally, even his at all. John McClaughry, at the time a youthful legislative aide to Senator Winston Prouty of Vermont and considered one of the brightest staff brains the Republicans had on Capitol Hill, had been toying with the thought for some time. "I sold Chuck that one," McClaughry recalled later. Percy, however, did have thoughts about low-income housing and the desirability of people owning their own homes. One Saturday in July, for example, campaigning around county fairs in northeastern Illinois, he talked with a reporter about ghetto housing. He was concerned about the problem, but he was thinking of it as something that belonged exclusively to the private sector.

"If a person owns a place, he is going to do more to keep it in good condition. He'll take more pride in it," he said. But he thought the answer to providing such housing lay in condominiums financed by insurance companies. To this end, he had written to a number of insurance executives, asking that they contribute ideas as to how their companies could participate in a scheme to make mortgages available to high-risk, low-income families.

The results of his letter-writing campaign had been "disappointing," he said. "They aren't moving as fast as I would like in this direction." The problem, of course, went back to his old view of business leadership as "a socially conscious community." The plain fact of the matter was that the insurance-company executives to whom he had written were not willing to involve their enterprises in a scheme which carried with it as many risks as were built into Percy's proposal to underwrite the least promising segment of American mortgage-seekers. No bank—or at least very few—would touch them. What Percy was in effect asking for was a commitment that the insurance companies, with obligations to make profits for their shareholders, would move into an area of utmost corporate risk.

Some other way, then, had to be found. The answer lay in McClaughry's program, whereby a nonprofit bank would be set up, with power to issue to the private sector bonds guaranteed by the federal government, to lend money to local organizations interested in providing one-owner or condominium or cooperative housing for ghetto residents. In principle, almost no federal money would be used for the project; the government's only role would be to guarantee the bonds, to urge private investors to put up the capital to move the project from the planning stage into reality.

This, then, was the way the National Home Ownership Foundation began to take shape, under McClaughry's prodding, in the summer of 1966. Percy was more than receptive to the idea. To him, it meant wedding private enterprise to government innovation. And the end result would be that some people—not all, but a significant number, of the nation's ghetto residents—would have private housing. It would, in Percy's and McClaughry's view, be a middle step, a transition from the high-rise public-housing vertical slums and dilapidated tenements to the suburbs, where the rest of America was going. And, indeed, it could spark model communities within the inner cities themselves, provide a check on the flight to the suburbs, and offer a chance for slum rehabilitation that would enhance taxes for the cities.

Beyond that, the program was by way of becoming the first reasonably progressive, reasonably broad piece of urban legislation the Republicans had put forth almost within the memory of living man.

On September 15, 1966, before the Kiwanis Club in Chicago, Percy described the NHOF plan as " a new dawn for our cities." Home ownership, he said, was both a product of and a means to encourage certain human values, among which were "human dignity and self-esteem, the motivation to achieve, a feeling of security and roots, community responsibility and stability, the physical preservation and improvement of residential neighborhoods and the encouragement of participation and leadership in community activities."

The concept was startling, in a way, particularly to an audience that held basically suburban values, the sort of men who constantly ask about ghetto Negroes, "Why can't they be more like us?" Here was a plan which would, in its mover's mind, answer that question affirmatively for some Negro families now living in slum conditions. It would, if it worked, give to the Negroes who were its beneficiaries some of the same suburban values that middle-class whites had.

Home ownership, the candidate said, could and should be made available to families whose present incomes and circumstances did not permit them to become homeowners. But research by Mc-Claughry and others had disclosed pitfalls. Pilot projects in other cities, including St. Louis and Philadelphia, had shown that you don't merely pluck a family out of a slum, give it a house and say, "Here, it's yours, now develop a sense of responsibility for private property." In one case, for example, copper plumbing had been ripped out of the walls by the owner to be sold. So some of the answer lay in education.

"A sound home-ownership program for initially lower-income families must contain a number of components designed to prepare the families for improving their economic security and accepting the responsibilities associated with home ownership," Percy said. These components, he went on to explain, included adult basic education, instruction in the simple skills and manners needed to seek employment, so that a steady income and steady mortgage payments would be insured. Initial descriptions of the plan also leaned heavily on job training and assistance in finding jobs. There was to be "counseling of the entire family in the responsibilities of home ownership, including financial obligations, insurance, taxes, home economics and credit buying"—the last two, particularly, being endemic symptoms of ghetto life. There should also be, Percy said, a program to encourage these putative middle-class families in the desirability of working with others in community projects, which would instill in them a sense of public service.

But, Percy told the Kiwanians, "the responsibility for conducting a national program of home ownership for initially lower-income families should lie with the nongovernmental sector, including both private enterprise and nonprofit organizations and groups. The role of government should only be one of reinforcement and guarantee, rather than execution and control."

The candidate also foresaw advantages to the cities in the plan, aside from merely helping slum dwellers to help themselves. He said emphasis should be placed not on individual, isolated dwellings, but on neighborhoods through neighborhood associations which already existed or which would be set up under the plan. There should be room in the legislation to provide for both new construction and rehabilitation of older housing.

The middle-class white American does not generally worry over-much about what might happen to him if he became ill for a time, or were laid off his job temporarily. There are sick-leave plans, union funds, health-insurance schemes—all of which are hedges against such temporary upheavals. Not so the ghetto Negro, who was the target of Percy's program. The initial beneficiaries of the home-ownership plan would be those living perilously close to the poverty mark—the family with an income of about $3,300 a year, with only $70 per month for housing. For such a family, whose head was probably not a member of any union and whose employer did not provide fat fringe benefits covering job security, even the most temporary dislocation of income could mean disaster. In his program, Percy foresaw that danger, too, and called for a nominal-cost insurance plan that would give some of the middle-class benefits to the lower-class families while they were finding their economic and social feet.

Percy did not, however, view his program as a panacea which, if enacted into law, would provide an immediate end to all the problems of the ghetto. "No feasible proposal can realistically promise to rebuild our cities and cure their accumulated social ills overnight," he said. "But a major effort should begin now to encourage a rapid acceleration of new activity in this field, especially by the nongovernmental sector of the economy."

At the heart of the proposal was the National Home Ownership Foundation, Inc., a private, nonprofit corporation established by act of Congress. "Since NHOF would have the benefit of certain government guarantees, tax advantages and delegated obligational authority, its corporate charter would provide for some public participation through the appointment of one-third of the board of directors by the President of the United States, with the advice and consent of the Senate," Percy said. "The remaining directors would be national leaders drawn from the ranks of business, labor, foundations, universities and civic groups. Initially, these persons would be those who joined together as a steering committee for NHOF."

But it would not always be thus.

The War on Poverty had already struggled with the problem of local community leadership, trying to ascertain to what extent the middle-class, largely white planners and social workers should tell the poor what they needed and what was good for them. Under the Percy program, local community groups who would be doing business with NHOF would have a voice in establishing NHOF policies.

This would be done, Percy said, by the establishment of a "congress" made up of representatives of local groups, which would be analogous to the National Rivers and Harbors Congress in the U.S. or the nonprofit housing federation in Denmark. Then, as the staggered terms of NHOF directors began to expire, the "congress" would submit a list of names to the board and to the President of the United States so that local participation on the board would be assured. "Alternatively," Percy suggested, "the NHOF Board could propose a slate of directors to the National Home Ownership Congress. The Congress could then vote yes or no on each, similar to the system used in many states for the retention of Judges."

The functions of NHOF, as Percy saw them, would be manifold:

1. To encourage and assist in the formation by local citizens of Local Non-Profit Housing Associations (LNHAs). These groups would serve a city, a neighborhood or, in some cases envisioned, a rural area.

2. To give the LNHAs technical assistance in setting up their program, to serve as a clearinghouse for information and research and to pass along lessons learned by other LNHAs.

3. To train personnel to assist the LNHAs, from executives to graduate-school-level interns.

4. To assist the local groups and local contractors with whom the LNHAs were working to find financing through loans and grants—not for housing itself, but for such prosaic things as telephone bills, office space, technical instruction and particularly know-how.

5. To make direct loans from a Home Ownership Loan Fund to qualified local groups for the rehabilitation or construction of low-cost housing for sale to families taking part in the local groups' ownership-orientation programs.

6. To use its authority to channel funds from existing government programs such as the Office of Economic Opportunity's Community Action program, Small Business Administration, Adult Basic Education, Manpower Development and Training and other agencies. This was a bold step indeed, since it meant that the proposed new organization would have obligational authority to use government-

agency funds on its own initiative. It was to cause wailing and gnashing of teeth in the upper echelon of existing administration offices.

7. To help the local groups to apply directly for such aid.

How was all this to be financed? It was quite simple, in Percy's view. If the ordinary commercial money outlets could not finance such a venture on their own because of the risks involved, then they could finance it by buying debenture bonds guaranteed by the federal government. The buyers, the program foresaw, would be commercial lending institutions, such as banks, savings and loan associations, and insurance companies. In addition, the bonds would be offered, at a rate of interest competitive with prime commercial bonds of equal term, to union pension and retirement funds, businesses, endowment funds set up by universities and religious groups and federal, state and local public bodies and agencies.

Initially, under the draft proposal, it would be the federal government which would buy bonds in amounts figured by Percy to range somewhere between $20 million and $100 million. These funds would provide what the candidate called "seed money capital" for immediate loans to LNHAs who qualified for them—in other words, a demonstration program to encourage other programs. The bonds would be tax-exempt, but the federal government, it was envisioned, would be able to recover the tax income lost through the participating families' either going onto the income-tax rolls or so improving their income that they would pay higher taxes.

What the scheme did, then, was basically to set up a bank aimed at helping members of low-income groups to acquire homes through federal guarantees of privately sold bonds; establish a technical-assistance branch to help local groups, such as, for example, the Woodlawn Organization in Chicago, which has worked for a dozen years on the South Side and has a record of success in community-action programs; and set up a finder service to aid the same organizations in locating private and public grants to educate and orient slum dwellers in home ownership, credit counseling and money management.

Many of the details spelled out here were not completely set by the time Percy first discussed his "new dawn for our cities" in his speech to the Kiwanians. But it was a major Percy program, and

McClaughry, working much of the time in a Chicago hotel room, was supplying refinements and details and delineations all through the fall.

Curiously enough, the program for low-income private ownership was not much of a campaign "issue" as such. Percy referred to it perhaps a dozen times between September and Election Day, but generally to civic groups at luncheons or in speeches in the ghetto, where he limited himself to the program's broad concepts rather than elaborating on details. The reason for this was obvious. In the heat of a campaign, there was too little time and too little interest in details on the part of voters, although his staff aides found there was considerable enthusiasm for the plan when it was discussed. But it was greeted with loud cries of delight by the influential members of the business community.

The plan had come a long way from the first discussions that July day in Lake County, when Percy talked about his disappointment in not getting cooperation from insurance companies, to the speech to the Kiwanians in September. By the time Percy got to Washington, he and McClaughry were ready to roll, and roll they did.

CHAPTER *13*

The Issues:
Housing—The Action

When the Ninetieth Congress convened on January 10, 1967, the House of Representatives, in a blaze of self-righteousness, created headlines and headaches by voting overwhelmingly, after hours of speech-making, to suspend Representative Adam Clayton Powell, the Harlem Democrat who had been accused of playing fast and loose with funds belonging to the House Committee on Education and Labor, of which he was chairman. It was a day of wild accusations and wilder emotions; the previous day, Monday, the Democratic caucus had voted to strip Powell of his chairmanship and his seniority, but this was not enough apparently.

Over on the Senate side, things were somewhat more sedate. The upper house, like a brontosaurus moving through primeval ooze, or like a royal progress, depending on which way one chose to look on it, was quietly beginning to go about the business of government. But Percy, one of five freshman Republican Senators, had not been in any mood to wait upon the Senate's very deliberate speed in accomplishing things. He had his housing program and he wanted to get it into the statute books in this first session of the Ninetieth Congress, and he wasted no time in lobbying for its early consideration.

He already had one advantage. The committee assignments for the five GOP freshmen were, in general, about what was to be ex-

135

pected, except for one assignment which Percy drew. That was a seat on the Banking and Currency Committee, the Senate body which would handle the housing bill after it had been put in final draft form and introduced. This would give him a chance to ride close herd on it at firsthand, without having to depend on help from another Senator who would have to be persuaded to carry the ball for him in the committee. It would also give him a chance, when hearings began, personally to question witnesses before the committee.

But Percy and those Republican Senators who were particularly interested in his future—especially Thruston Morton—wanted more than that; they wanted to find the broadest kind of support for the bill even before it was introduced. Thus Percy had his first lesson in how to lobby and chivy and persuade. He scored an initial success by getting the plan, even without a direct reference to it as his bill, included in the Republican "State of the Union" message, delivered by Percy's fellow Illinoisan, Senator Dirksen, and House GOP leader Representative Gerald R. Ford of Michigan. In this message, which followed by a few days President Johnson's State of the Union speech, there was a reference to the desirability of low-income families being able to own their own homes. This was enough; the Percy housing bill had become a Republican program bill.

Members of more senior GOP Senators' staffs were amazed. No one, at least no one that anyone could recall, had ever succeeded in persuading the party Congressional leadership to make a program bill out of a piece of legislation—not yet even in draft stage— proposed by a freshman Senator. It just wasn't done. Besides, to these staff members, if not to the Senators they served, Percy was already becoming just a little bit of a figure of fun. "Pushy" was the word used most often, and the tone was similar to that used in preparatory schools to denigrate a "fresh new boy" who pays little attention to the customs of the school and the deference due those who have been there a longer time. "My God, he comes on strong!" exclaimed the administrative assistant of a Western Republican senior Senator a few weeks after Congress convened.

One minor incident is illustrative. GOP Senator Jacob K. Javits and Democratic Senator Robert F. Kennedy of New York had earlier achieved passage of legislation which in some areas apparently paralleled Percy's housing bill. The New York Senators called for urban-renewal and slum-clearance projects to concentrate, wherever and whenever possible, on establishing condominium and private housing. It did not set up an organism similar to the National Home Ownership Foundation to administer such projects, but there were some similarities and overlaps. Therefore it became desirable for Percy to gain Javits' support for the Percy program, if possible. One of Percy's top aides went to Javits' staff and suggested a joint press conference in Percy's office, at which Percy would outline, briefly, his own plan, and then introduce Javits to the assembled reporters so that the New York Republican could explain that the apparent overlap was not what it seemed and that Percy's program was, in Javits' view, a very sound piece of legislation.

The Percy staffer who made the suggestion went on his way after making it, but the Javits staff, when they could stop laughing, were more or less aghast. Imagine the idea of *Percy*, the freshman, introducing *Javits*, the veteran, to the Washington press corps! The story was too good to keep under wraps, and it rapidly went the rounds of the Senate press gallery. But it should be noted that Javits became one of Percy's strongest supporters as time went by.

Percy's arrival in the Senate, with or without the housing program, was not all laughing up sleeves, however. Among some of the younger, more progressive Republicans his hell-for-leather approach, tempered with good manners and a considerable degree of deference, won him admirers. One GOP staff member told a reporter: "Chuck Percy would probably be remiss if he did not push ahead with his programs instead of waiting for archaic tradition to catch up."

The housing bill was already attracting attention from Democrats, too, and it had not yet even been put in circulation-draft form by McClaughry. While Percy was trying to build support for it—in earnest sales talks to individual Senators and at a lunch of the Republican Policy Committee in mid-January—Democratic urbanists were looking at what they could find out about the bill with a hard eye.

"It's a well-intentioned proposal," said one Democratic staff member who had had a hand in drafting some of his party's major anti-poverty legislation. "The trouble is, though, that it doesn't attack the real problem in the slums, which is jobs. It's great for people who have jobs, and are getting ready to move into the stratum of the Negro middle class in the cities, but it doesn't affect enough people for the amount of effort that will be put into it, and it doesn't provide jobs. Without jobs no one can have decent housing. I hope the idea isn't to have people take their mortgage payments out of welfare checks."

What the Democratic staffer was doing was to express an argument familiar to all students of urban affairs and a question that is almost as unanswerable as which came first, the chicken or the egg. Is the real root problem of the ghetto jobs, or housing, or education? It is certainly all three, but which is to be attacked first?

"Percy's proposal is practical in a great many respects," said the Democrat, "but a new dawn for our cities it ain't."

When McClaughry heard this particular piece of criticism, he reacted like a mother lioness. "That's just not true," he said. "There are very definite proposals to upgrade the income level of people who qualify for home ownership under the program. It's an integral part of the plan."

And so it went. Since McClaughry had not finished polishing a draft bill to be shown to other GOP Senators, the information on it that the Democratic staff members were receiving was inclined to be secondhand or incomplete, or both. McClaughry and Percy found themselves defending the bill and its provisions against attacks which were not always based on the best reports available. By March, however, McClaughry had put together a draft bill, and now it began to move from Republican Senator to Republican Senator. Staff members dissected it, tore it apart, made suggestions and comments and in general liked what they saw.

"I'm having the best darned time with this housing bill," Percy told a visitor in April, shortly before its formal introduction. "People —Senators and their staffs—have been so helpful in getting it into final form. It really is wonderful to see how interested everyone is in it."

Interested was an understatement. Administration agencies, well aware of the measure's potential were also trying to find out exactly what the provisions were and how they would be carried out. In the end, when it was being readied for formal presentation, the Percy staff had to take elaborate security precautions to make sure that only a small number of people saw the proposed law in its final form. In all legislative bodies, and particularly on Capitol Hill, bill-stealing—the practice of sneaking a draft measure away from the opposition and introducing it first—is a time-honored custom.

By mid-April the initial sculpture had been accomplished, the suggestions considered worthwhile had been incorporated into the original draft, and the time had come for introduction, which itself was only the beginning of a long fight in committee. Percy had a speaking engagement before the Washington Urban League on the night of April 19, and he decided to use the speech to discuss the bill which he would introduce the next day.

He noted that the 1966 annual report of the League had called housing "the most critical" of all urban problems. "If the housing needs of today's slum dwellers are to be effectively met," he said, "we must find a way to bridge the credit gap. Hard data are difficult to come by, but I am sure that any of you who have worked in the housing field instinctively know that mortgage financing and home-improvement loans can be desperately hard to obtain in areas that lenders regard as a slum." The result of lack of available credit, Percy said, "is the further deterioration of the ghetto. If our urban ghettos are to be revitalized as decent, attractive communities—and they must be—some way must be found to bring more credit in on reasonable terms to do the job."

When he had first advanced the idea of private housing for low-income families, Percy said, "I spoke in terms of outright sale to poor families because I believed then—and believe even more strongly now—that home ownership can be a powerful force for motivating them to invest in themselves—to rise through their efforts to economic security."

He acknowledged the help he had had from fellow Republicans in the Congress in drafting the legislation: "The bill I intend to introduce tomorrow represents a tremendous improvement over the first version advanced last fall." And he said that both GOP and Democratic members of the Senate Housing Subcommittee of the Banking and Currency Committee, which would be working on the bill, could offer "further refinement."

"I am fully aware that this legislation is not perfect," he said. "I am aware that it does not provide the answer to *all* our slum housing problems or new hope to *all* slum people. But it is a beginning."

He quoted President Johnson, who, speaking on urban problems before the Brookings Institution in Washington the previous September, had said: "We need not delay action in the cities until Brookings, and its sister institutions, have given us a definite answer. . . . When governments are faced with great public dilemmas, they must shape their programs with the greatest wisdom that they possess, but governments must act. They cannot wait to act until all that is tentative and hypothetical can be established as firmly as a law of mathematics." That, Percy said, "is the spirit in which I will offer this legislation tomorrow. That is the spirit in which I hope it will be received." He said that he hoped the National Home Ownership Foundation would become a reality, and added that "when it is, we will have an important new tool for mobilizing the enormous resources of the private sector behind sound grass-roots programs to make today's poor slum families the middle-income homeowners of tomorrow."

On April 20, Senate Bill 1592 and its identical companion measure, House Bill 8820, were introduced with accompanying memoranda inserted in the *Congressional Record*. The administration wasted no time in flaying the Percy proposals. Robert C. Weaver, Secretary of Housing and Urban Development, issued a nine-page statement on April 21 which attacked the program on several grounds. The Percy proposal, he said, "fails to involve local governments," would be inadequate to aid lower-income families buy homes despite an "incalculable" cost to the taxpayer, "fails to provide adequately for the relocation of people who may be displaced," and subsidies would be needed to provide insurance against homeowners losing their homes because of temporary economic reversals.

Some weeks later Weaver made an even more dramatic thrust at the bill. Appearing on a television interview program, the Secretary was asked his opinion of the Percy program. "I think to promise large numbers of low-income people that in the immediate future they are going to be able to receive home ownership is a snare and a delusion, and it can be a cruel hoax, because in many instances, with these extremely low down payments, with these long periods of loans, after three years they will have a negative equity. So if they lose their jobs, or if they are sick, they will lose their homes. And if you think you have disillusionment and you think you have despair and potential violence in the ghetto now, what's going to happen if this occurs in large numbers?"

Weaver conceded that under an administration home-ownership program which had recently been initiated through the 1966 Housing and Redevelopment Act, there was still some danger that home-owners might find their mortgages foreclosed, but he said that the potential for violence was less because the administration program was less ambitious, in terms of numbers, than the Percy proposals were.

The view rightly taken by Percy was that the Weaver reaction to the newly introduced bill represented official administration dogma on the National Home Ownership Foundation and should be answered as such, in detail and without passion. The staff study and reply took two months to prepare, and when it came, it was a sixteen-page "factual analysis" of Weaver's April statement, issued as a press release. Where Weaver had said that that NHOF "failed to involve local governments," the Percy staff cited ten points in the bill and memorandum which referred to the involvement of local agencies, private, public and quasi-public.

The Percy memorandum also defended the bill on the other grounds which Weaver had used as a basis for attack. Cost, the memorandum said, would be far from "incalculable"; there were provisions in the bill governing relocation of persons displaced by a local group seeking to acquire property; insurance against fore-closure could be written, according to experts in the field, for something on the order of $25 in annual premiums.

As its conclusion, the Percy memorandum quoted Weaver's original statement, which said the administration

welcomes interest in urban development and the rebuilding of declining urban and rural areas. We are encouraged, too, by the fact that there is agreement between the Administration and the supporters of this proposal in certain basic goals. All of us are dedicated to maximum involvement of private enterprise in housing and urban development and the increase of home ownership opportunity among low-income families. As the proposal is being considered by the Congress, we hope that its analysis will afford the basis for a bipartisan support of effective legislation in this vital aspect of domestic life.

The Percy memo ended by crying amen to that statement, saying that the sponsors of the bill (all the GOP Senators and 110 of the 187 House Republicans) "find themselves in strong accord with these constructive remarks."

The Senate's Housing Subcommittee, in the weeks that followed introduction of the Percy bill, found itself inundated with a number of bills in the private-ownership-for-low-income-housing field. Some of them, like that drafted by Senator Walter Mondale, Democrat of Minnesota, bore a strong resemblance to the Percy bill. Others called for different approaches to the problem. Through the summer and into the fall, Percy and Mrs. Carol Khosrovi, a legislative assistant who had worked closely with McClaughry, met to try to draft a bill which would include as many aspects as possible of the bill introduced by the Illinois freshman—and a freshman, too, who was becoming more and more talked about as a possible opponent to President Johnson the following year.

"Let's face it," said one top Republican Senate staff member in the fall of 1967, "it might very well be that the gentleman at 1600 Pennsylvania Avenue has already put out the word that we ain't doing no favors for Chuck Percy this year."

The Percy housing bill was swallowed up in a welter of other measures in an omnibus bill, which was reported out of committee but not taken up on the floor in the closing days of the first session of the Ninetieth Congress.

In the omnibus bill were provisions for private ownership of low-income housing, but lost in the shuffle was the Home Ownership Foundation, which had been at the heart of the measure. But it was due for another look as the second session got under way in January, 1968.

Percy, during this time, was inclined to take a philosophical view of the pushing and hauling on his bill. "You know," he told an interviewer while the bill was in committee, "I used to have a sign in my office at Bell & Howell that said: 'There's no limit to what a man can accomplish if he doesn't care who gets the credit.' It doesn't matter a great deal whether it's the Percy bill or not, as long as some poor people have housing. That's what I'm after."

That was a commendable attitude for a businessman, but a little less than practical for a politician. It hardly made any difference, however. Percy had managed, in his first year as a Senator, to link his name with a major program bill for his party, a major piece of urban legislation and, quite possibly, an excellent issue for the party and for himself in the 1968 Presidential campaign. The urban voter in 1967 was beginning to be more and more wooed by the GOP and a Percy housing bill could certainly do no harm, politically, and might do a great deal of good.

CHAPTER *14*

The Issues:
Vietnam—"The Seven Failures"

By the end of 1964 it had become apparent to Americans that Vietnam was bulking very large in their lives and would undoubtedly bulk larger. During the Presidential campaign, Senator Goldwater had castigated President Johnson for not doing enough to ensure victory, and the President had countered with the answer that the mission of the United States was to pursue limited goals, to halt what the President called the "aggression" by Hanoi and to ensure the stability and survival of the government of the Republic of South Vietnam, to which Washington was bound by treaty.

Percy, again a private man but with the prospect of a Senate campaign already somewhat on his mind, decided after the elections to go and take a look for himself and, within the limitations imposed on him by his private status, to try to formulate his own ideas on what could be done to bring peace to Southeast Asia.

He toured the countries of that area and met with many of their leaders. "What became apparent to me," he said later in an interview, "was that the Asians themselves were playing such a small role in the defense of their own area. We were committing more and more men and matériel, while the Asians were doing comparatively little. We needed, I felt, to have more Asian support and help."

But Percy had not only talked to Asian leaders; he had also seen the fighting zones at firsthand. Before taking off on his first helicopter tour of the combat zone, he recalled later, he was handed a flak vest, which he started to put on in the regulation manner. "No," said the pilot, "we don't wear them that way. Sit on it; that's where the bullets come from."

On his return, Percy went to Washington to talk to Secretary of Defense Robert S. McNamara. What he had in mind particularly was to ask why some persuasion could not be exercised on Thailand. Percy had talked to that country's Foreign Minister, Thanat Khoman, and had received the impression that Thanat, more than most other Asian officials, would be willing to use his influence in his government to help bring about an end to the war. He got short shrift from McNamara, who took the attitude that it would be unwise to expect the Thais to do a great deal, since they had internal problems which might exacerbate rather than improve the situation.

The basic problem, of course, was the menace of Communist China, which, if there was too much of a concerted effort by the other countries of Southeast Asia, might decide to take a more active hand in the fighting than it had hitherto taken.

As a private citizen, there was little Percy could do to influence the government on Vietnam. Indeed, about the only thing that could be done, he did—began preparing a position for himself if he decided to run for the Senate. New Illinois Committee staff members worked on some research on Vietnam, for example.

But when the campaign got under way, Percy was sure, as was Houser, that Vietnam would be a major issue. In the early weeks of the race, there was uncertainty as to exactly what sort of tack should be taken, but still uppermost in Percy's mind was the question of Asian participation—in the fighting or in the pursuit of a peace settlement. "I felt we really couldn't commit an unlimited amount of effort in Vietnam," he said in an interview in 1967, "and I also believed that there had been points reached where negotiations could have been possible if we had taken the opportunity at the time."

Publicly, he was saying that "as the United States escalates its military efforts, it should be escalating its efforts to find a peaceful solution." And in campaign speeches he was attacking the "credibility gap" which he, along with many other Americans—candidates or not—felt the administration had created. "If there is a credibility gap in the United States today, it results from the astonishing lack of candor shown by the Executive Branch in regard to Vietnam," he said in Elgin in April. "From the very beginning, the American public has been confused as it has tried to understand the war in Vietnam—confused about our aims, our tactics, our progress.

"Much of this confusion is the fault of government officials. They have obscured and distorted the news from Vietnam, and they have misled us with erroneous evaluations of the war's progress. In 1963 we were told by the White House that no Americans were fighting in Vietnam. Yet, as early as 1962, it was evident to all observers on the scene that the United States was involved in undeclared war in Vietnam. It was well known to the Russians, to the Chinese Communists and to everyone else concerned, except the American people."

The candidate questioned why it was that administration officials "insist on perpetuating the myth for so long that we were participating in Vietnam merely as 'advisers.'" And he asked why, "until very recently, were we continually told that everything was going just fine, despite reports to the contrary by newsmen at the scene?

"What is happening, of course—although we are not told it in so many words—is a steady build-up of American forces. This may not be considered escalation by the Pentagon, but to students facing increased draft calls, to the American people facing increasing casualty lists, the semantics of the situation are unimportant. What *is* important is that the American public start getting the facts, and getting them straight. America is at war today in Vietnam— make no mistake about it. We are largely responsible for directing the war. Americans are being killed in the war. American money is financing the war. I insist that the American people have the right to know everything about the war, except information which might impair the military effort."

Three weeks later, President Johnson, who was beginning to be stung by criticism of the war—now coming not only from a handful of disaffected Democratic "intellectuals" and from Republicans who could smell a good political issue, but from a growing cross section of the country—came to Chicago to make a speech. In it, he took the trouble to answer some of his critics, and called them "nervous Nellies." Two days later, Percy shifted his attack on the conduct of the war from the vague target of "administration officials" to the President himself.

"He's darn right we're nervous," Percy told a group of newspaper editors in Quincy. "The American people are nervous. And from every indication, we're going to become more nervous." He attacked administration "deception" in the handling of the issue of free elections in South Vietnam, and said: "Two weeks ago, Premier Ky indicated that if the proposed free elections in South Vietnam should result even in a neutralist government, he and his followers would fight that government. Since our government has enthusiastically embraced Ky and has pledged itself to abide by free elections, no matter what the outcome, the Premier's blunt remarks were obviously embarrassing to the administration."

Then he laid his lash onto Secretary of State Dean Rusk, who had said Nguyen Cao Ky had been "misunderstood." The only trouble was that Ky, in one of the rare instances in which a politician has "clarified" earlier remarks without making them more murky, left no question that those who had heard him the first time heard him right. If a Constituent Assembly which Ky did not like were elected in Vietnam, he said, he and his backers would "stand and fight."

Percy said that Rusk's remarks were "a clumsy attempt to cover up the truth. . . . The administration says that one of its goals in Vietnam is free elections. At the same time, the administration supports a premier who is opposed to this goal. And finally, we have a Secretary of State who clumsily tries to cloud this contradiction in policy. In such circumstances, is it any wonder, Mr. President, that Americans are nervous about the conduct of the war?"

Later in the year, and in 1967, the terms "hawk" and "dove," as applied to many of the citizens of Illinois, tended to fade, to become more fuzzy, to be replaced by an almost universal feeling that *something* was going terribly wrong with the war, that the most powerful nation in the world, for reasons that were escaping the ordinary voter, somehow could neither win the war nor extricate itself from it. Just what the people of Illinois wanted done was not clear, but they wanted out, and wanted out badly. At the time Percy was talking, in the spring of 1966, however, the public-opinion polls were showing a far more hawkish trend than a dovish one. Although people were confused—and Percy was touching a responsive chord with his attacks on the President—Illinoisans, nevertheless, wanted a victory.

In addition to his attacks on the President and the administration for confusing the people, Percy was also appealing to voters on the grounds that the administration was not doing enough, on a diplomatic level, to persuade America's free world allies that they could at least help by not trading with North Vietnam.

"I believe the administration should do everything feasible to end our allies' continuing breach of loyalty, and to end it soon," Percy told a veterans' group in Salem in June. "Additionally, we should seek to reduce tonnage going into Haiphong. Elimination of free world ships going to North Vietnam would undoubtedly reduce the total amount of goods flowing to the enemy."

This was a tricky issue, and Percy was careful about when and how he referred to it. The United Kingdom, for example, provided through its trade with North Vietnam an excellent listening post for Washington; to reduce or eliminate the efficacy of diplomatic channels between Hanoi and the East would have been at least difficult, if not disastrous. But allied "disloyalty" was a recurring campaign theme.

Beyond that, however, it was becoming more and more evident that these two arguments—public confusion and trade with the enemy—were not going to make a solid political issue for a campaign in which Percy's opponent, one of the Senate's great Cold Warriors, would be sure to take a hard line against any efforts to secure a settlement through signing away military and political objectives. Something wider, something "constructive," was indicated.

The question of increased Asian involvement was being worked on by researchers, polished and honed down into a final position paper, but by the end of June it was by no means certain that it was going to form an important part of the Percy stand on Vietnam.

On June 28, in Percy's campaign headquarters office in Chicago, a full-dress strategy session was held to discuss what the approach should be toward Vietnam. Some at the conference held that a hard line should be taken, a demand for early military victory to bring Hanoi to the conference table by force of arms; others said that to start negotiations on any basis, without further escalation, would be the best way to bring the war to an end. The split in the strategy meeting was typical of the split in the state and in the country, and it was a split that was crossing party lines.

What emerged was the concept of an "all-Asian peace conference," a plan under which all nations concerned would be invited to meet to discuss and suggest ways to end the war. In the original draft there were specific ideas that the conference should consist of foreign ministers and that the President of the United States summon the conference. But, it was argued, to say that such a meeting must be on the ministerial level might produce too much hardened thinking at the outset and reduce the conference's potential effectiveness. It was also argued that for the President to call the conference would detract from a basic aim of the proposal: that the Asian nations themselves, since it was their part of the world that was concerned, should decide on the mechanics of the meeting. The final suggestion was that U Thant, Secretary General of the United Nations, would be an ideal person to be the convener of an Asian meeting, both because he was a Burmese himself and because of his international prestige.

Above all, however, the conference was to exclude no one in the area—including Communist China—and the United States would be present only as an observer.

While campaign aides were preparing the final draft of the statement, for presentation at a press conference, President Johnson on June 30 ordered the bombing of targets around Hanoi and Haiphong. The action gave Percy and his strategists what they basically needed —a peg on which to hang their proposals.

On July 2 Percy called a press conference in Chicago and read the statement calling for the all-Asian conference:

> America's escalation of the war in Vietnam in recent days makes it imperative that we now quicken and intensify our efforts to seek a just peace. By bombing within 900 yards of a large civilian center, we have multiplied the risk of this war—the risk of Chinese intervention, the risk of enemy escalation, the risk of still more casualties among innocent men, women and children. If we must accelerate the war—as the Administration believes we must— then let us also accelerate the pursuit of peace.
>
> As we all know, the enemy has indicated that he is not prepared to negotiate directly with the United States. Therefore, I urge a new approach to end this tragic war.
>
> I earnestly suggest that a conference of all Asian nations be called to work toward a settlement of the Vietnam war. I further suggest that such a conference could be called by U Thant, Secretary General of the United Nations. Himself an Asian, U Thant

enjoys the confidence of both East and West, and would exert an influence clearly free of national self-interest.

An All-Asian "peacemaking" conference would allow those most directly endangered to deal directly with the problem at hand. Its recommendations would reflect an understanding of the region which is essential to the restoration of peace. It would serve to find an Asian solution to a problem in Asia which threatens the peace of the world.

No one could guarantee the success of such a conference, but it is an approach worth trying. Perhaps an Asian conference would be only a beginning. But let us begin.

Politically, the concept and the statement were superlatively conceived and superlatively worded, not only in what was said, but in what was not said. It was a new idea, and it suggested doing *something* in addition to escalating the war, and that something, incidentally, would not cost the American taxpayer a dime. To those who were weary of having Americans slogging through the paddy fields and jungles of a far-off land about which most people could not work up a high degree of enthusiasm, it left the initiative for settling the conflict in the hands of the Asians, who had not, for various reasons, been doing very much about this war anyway.

There was no overt criticism of the U.S. military role in Vietnam, and the statement merely said that if the administration was going to heighten the U.S. military involvement, somebody ought to do something about bringing about peace at the same time. It did not suggest a unilateral American withdrawal or even a bombing halt. Nor did it suggest that the United States would be committed to abiding by whatever the Asians might decide was the best course to end the war. U Thant would call the conference and the Asian nations themselves would decide whom they would invite; if they wanted Peking there, then it did not mean that the United States necessarily wanted Peking there. While not an innocuous statement, it was extremely hard to punch any large holes in it, as the Democrats were to discover.

And who could mistake the Kennedyesque ring of that final sentence: ". . . let us begin"?

Now the proposal was made and on the table, and the problem was to keep it alive, to get a national push behind it, from as many influential people as possible. A prime mover in this area was to be Thruston Morton, the Kentucky-born Yale graduate who had emerged as a principal spokesman for the moderate GOP wing of the Senate in foreign affairs. Morton was already a close associate of Percy's in the race, making a dozen trips to Illinois to advise and campaign for him ("I like winners," he said later). He also loaned Percy his press aide, Duff Reed, thirty-seven, a long-time Washington publicity man who had been New York Senator Kenneth Keating's press spokesman in Keating's ill-starred 1964 campaign for re-election, which he lost to Robert Kennedy. With Morton's blessing and help, Reed began beating the drums for the all-Asian peace conference.

On July 19 Morton read Percy's statement into the *Congressional Record,* calling it "the type of imaginative thinking desperately needed, in and out of government, if our goals [in Vietnam] are to be realized." He suggested that the newly organized Asia and Pacific Council might be the body to launch a new peace offensive along the lines suggested by Percy. This group consisted of South Korea, the Philippines, Thailand, Japan, Australia, New Zealand, Taiwan, Malaysia and South Vietnam. Laos had observer status in the Council.

In his speech on the Senate floor, Morton paraphrased Percy's words when he said that the increased bombing around Hanoi and Haiphong, which he had suggested in January, presented "a mounting danger today that continued military escalation without an equal acceleration of peace-seeking efforts may well result in the eventual negotiations over a wasteland."

On August 1 Morton, the chairman of the Republican Senatorial Campaign Committee, sent out to all GOP Senate candidates a suggested statement which called for an all-Asian conference. And on August 3 there came the hoped-for reaction from the Asians themselves; Thant endorsed the proposal. The snowball was beginning to grow larger; most major political columnists dwelt at length on the prospect for the conference, naming Percy as its author.

Early in August former President Eisenhower said the proposal was "worthy of serious consideration. Even if such an effort, held under such respectable auspices, should fail to uncover any new possibilities for furthering such an objective, the effort would still be a worthy one." And former Vice President Nixon called an Asian-produced settlement "the best way to end the war in Vietnam."

Even President Johnson, without of course mentioning Percy, said the idea had considerable merit.

What was happening—especially after Thant's proposal—was that the plan for an Asian conference was becoming more and more associated with Percy. Republican Senator after Republican Senator fell into line and pushed for the conference, and each mentioned the GOP Senatorial candidate in Illinois.

While Percy was in California following Valerie's murder, in late September came the announcement that the President would go to Manila as part of a "peace offensive" for Vietnam and would meet there with Asian leaders. Early in October the Percy campaign strategists tried to calculate ways to deal with this widely publicized trip, which eventually included a visit to the fighting men in Vietnam itself.

They believed—as did others—that the polls were showing that further escalation moves were not meeting with the earlier approval of such moves by the voters, and that another approach was needed. Also, the earlier thinking among the Democrats nationally that the 1966 campaign should be a reflection of public confidence in the administration conduct of the war was not turning out that way; nearly all the contests across the nation were not between "war" and "peace" candidates, but between two adversaries who more or less approved of the war effort. But among Democratic Congressmen there was a fall-off of sentiment in favor of the war, and to force them into a position of all-out support might hurt their chances.

A confidential campaign memorandum prepared for Houser in October read the signs in this manner:

> The current "peace offensive" will permit President Johnson to influence (for him, hopefully, in a positive way) the elections without actually participating in them. Thus, any losses which are incurred will not really reflect a repudiation of the President himself. By following this course, he can also avoid having to answer criticisms of his economic and foreign policies. By timing the "peace offensive" to reach its zenith just a few days before the election, the fact that it may well be a failure will not be fully realized by the electorate until after the election.

To offset the President's trip, the Percy forces suggested that the Manila trip merely was a military briefing session for leaders of allied nations combined with a courtesy call to friendly capitals. But the candidate did not lean too hard on the issue; for one thing, if the Manila conference was to be a success, and the President were able, a few days before elections, to pull a dove of peace from his political hat with a momentous pronouncement on a new and relatively unassailable solution to the war, then the charges would ring somewhat hollow. Also, the campaign was building toward the downstate trip, and the concentration was on issues which would particularly interest downstate voters. The war, with its mounting casualties and what Percy called "the inflation born of a war economy," were important, but only part of what the big, final push was to be.

The all-Asian peace conference was causing Douglas some headaches as well. He described it in various speeches and statements as "a meeting at which Red China will be present but the United States won't be," and the inference could be drawn that Peking would dictate the terms for Southeast Asian peace, largely by the threat of its huge size and might. Douglas' problem was that the idea, whatever its merits, was ephemeral; the limitations on the conference would be imposed by the Asians themselves and the original statement was so drafted that it omitted any binding commitment on the part of the United States. Also, the leader of the Democratic party, President Johnson, had approved the conference in principle.

In addition to all this, Douglas was to thunder up and down the state that "I am not a war hawk," and the operative word was "not." Having to deny something is the most uncomfortable position into which a political candidate can be maneuvered. Douglas stood for the continuation of the administration military effort in Vietnam; he believed fervently that the United States had commitments in Vietnam which had to be honored, and he stuck by that position, although Percy made it tougher and tougher for him to do so.

As the campaign was drawing to a close, Douglas gave Percy another opening on Vietnam by suggesting on a nationwide television broadcast that the possibility should not be ruled out that it might be possible to use tactical nuclear weapons against enemy soldiers in the field. It was unfortunate for Douglas because it raised the specter of nuclear war in a conflict which was bad enough as a conventional war.

Percy, in a reply from his Chicago office, said that "even to suggest initiating the use of nuclear weapons of any size in a limited war is irresponsible. It is irresponsible because this would challenge the Communist nations to respond with nuclear weapons of their own. To initiate the use of nuclear weapons, no matter how small, no matter what the target, would open the door to nuclear warfare. It is irresponsible because in Vietnam it is impossible to target nuclear weapons only against uniformed troops. Inevitably, innocent civilians would be killed, even as they are being killed today by conventional weapons. We are not in Vietnam to destroy that country or its people or to invite nuclear retaliation on our own boys. We are there to save the country."

A week later, on his downstate train trip, Percy returned to the bugbear, the scare issue, of nuclear weapons in Vietnam. In a speech at Alton he reiterated his earlier remarks and said that "the entire world lives on the brink of annihilation." Yet he said, "Senator Douglas regards nuclear warfare so casually that he called for atom bombing of China during the Korean War and the use of small nuclear weapons against uniformed forces in the field in Vietnam." (This was an exaggerated statement on both counts; Douglas never went further than to say the use of nuclear weapons might be considered.)

By the time Percy went to the Senate, the all-Asian peace conference had gone to join a number of other proposed suggestions for maneuvers on the diplomatic front, such as the President's call for a Soviet united front, so to speak, with the West to bring about peace, and a meeting of Soviet and North Vietnamese leaders on the Black Sea, which was supposed to produce an alienation of Hanoi from Peking. More than two months before the elections, Harrison E. Salisbury wrote in the *New York Times* that

It is not very likely that the proposed all-Asian conference to settle the Vietnam war will bring peace to Southeast Asia. Indeed, even though President Johnson has given it his blessing, it will be a surprise if the meeting even comes about. Nonetheless, the call for the conference may well prove to be a most important development in that troubled part of the world—more important, even, than the United States escalation of the war or the weird

goings-on in Peking. . . [But among all the diplomatic develop-
ments] the most important in the opinion of those who follow
Asian affairs is the all-Asian conference suggestion. Its importance
lies in the fact that it represents an all-Asian initiative.

Thus, from the mind of a Middle Western businessman, not yet
even elected to the United States Senate, had come an idea and a
plan which had had, for all its long-range lack of success, a real
impact on international diplomacy. In addition to its political merits,
which were many, it had provided a talking point for those who were
seeking not merely military but diplomatic solutions for the war.
And for Percy himself, its national reverberations generally meant
that "All-Asian conference" inevitably called to mind Charles Percy.
For a freshman whose aim it was to stand tall in the foreign-policy
councils of his party, this was no small mark to have next to his
name.

The following winter and early spring in Washington saw, too, a
number of diplomatic maneuvers and hopes for peace raised and
dashed. There was a bombing halt and suggestions that it should
be continued. Robert Kennedy returned from talks with French diplomats in Paris with what appeared for a time to be a peace nibble;
others read similar signs in meetings between British Prime Minister
Harold Wilson and Soviet Premier Alexei Kosygin in London. The
word "negotiations" hung in the air, and whether the cold water was
thrown by Washington or Hanoi, it was thrown. Besides, on the
battleground itself the Vietcong and North Vietnamese armies were
tying down a huge American military machine—450,000 men maintained at a cost of nearly $30 billion a year. If Hanoi was intractable,
it was apparently because its planners felt they could afford to be,
that sooner or later the United States, drained of its blood and trea-
sure, would itself be suing for peace.

Percy had expressed himself in private conversation and in campaign speeches many times. Typical was a remark he made to an interviewer in January: "What we should do is announce to everyone
that we plan to have our people at some neutral point—Rangoon or
Cairo or somewhere—on such-and-such a date to talk about nearly
any issue. It could be the exchange of wounded prisoners, or steps
to demilitarize the Demilitarized Zone. But the point would be that
we were doing something concrete. If nothing came of it, at least
we would have taken the initiative in seeking to sit down and talk.

Let the other side look bad for a change. And if we could get them to talk, we could start small with an issue like that and then enlarge it."

Publicly, as a Senator, he began, too, to be more specific. On "Meet the Press" he had said that while the bombing of North Vietnam did not appear to be achieving much, it probably would be a good idea to continue until Hanoi came up with an offer that we could accept in exchange for cessation of bombing. In February, however, he had moved his position so that it would be Washington which would make the offer. "The prospects for negotiation would be better if we would now offer to end the bombing of North Vietnam as soon as negotiations begin. This cessation would not be unconditional, but would continue only so long as the North Vietnamese and Vietcong negotiate in good faith," he said in a Chicago speech.

He criticized the administration for "vague pronouncements" on American willingness to sit down at the table, and asked that a specific date be set, perhaps March 1, for opening talks, and said "this would serve both to prove our own genuine desire to negotiate and to test the enemy's interest in negotiating. Without a precise, defined invitation to open negotiations, we can expect no precise, defined response. Moreover, only by issuing a specific invitation to talk can the administration convince the world of our determination to end this war."

But, as Percy said later in a Washington speech, nothing was done and "the most propitious moment for such a move has passed us by. We must, therefore, look for other openings." The White House, State Department and Pentagon were not, however, painted by the Illinois freshman as the sole culprits in the failure to find a Vietnamese solution. There were the intractables in Hanoi and Peking and Moscow—and in the United States—who were helping to block a settlement.

"It is argued that any contact with Communist nations is a betrayal of American soldiers in Vietnam," Percy said in a Washington speech in April. "I cannot agree. I think we owe it to the men who must fight our wars to promote peace and peaceful contact in every way we can." But the first priority must be Vietnam, and to those who called for "total victory" in the war, he had this to say:

"We must remind them that already nine thousand American men have died there and we have suffered over 63,000 casualties. We must answer whether we are prepared to allow our men to die at the rate of two hundred to three hundred a month for an interminable number of years, in search of a total victory that cannot be achieved. I think that just as we fight a limited war, we must also have the wisdom to put limits on our expectations. We must limit our expectations to a settlement which gives assurance that the people of South Vietnam may determine their own future, free of North Vietnamese coercion. Such a settlement will require that the Vietcong be assured of participation in South Vietnamese political life as a legal political party competing peacefully at the polls and shunning violence. I have long felt that it has been unrealistic for Saigon—and therefore ourselves—to propose negotiations with Hanoi without inviting the Vietcong to fully participate if we truly hope to see negotiations come about in the foreseeable future. I cannot join with those who say that Hanoi's rejections of President Johnson's and U Thant's proposals for negotiations mean that negotiations are impossible."

But he took both the President and the Secretary General to task for ringing their proposals around with conditions that made it, in his view, impossible for the North Vietnamese to accept. As far as U Thant was concerned, his suggestion that the Geneva Conference of 1954 be reconvened would be unacceptable to the Communist Chinese because what would follow would amount to "overt Soviet mediation." At the same time, Percy said, President Johnson had "asked Hanoi virtually to abandon its forces in the South before the U.S. would end the bombing of the North. To ask Hanoi to end the resupply and reinforcement of its forces in the South is unrealistic."

Although these proposals had, at the time they were made, Percy said, "little chance of acceptance, at the same time, let it be said that if Hanoi wants peace, then Hanoi must share the task of making proposals which might lead to negotiation. Thus far, Hanoi's rigidity and bellicose statements have only diminished the chances for peace. And if the leaders in Hanoi were at all sensitive to American public opinion, they would realize that such an attitude could only strengthen the hand of those who would press the President into higher and higher escalation of America's military effort."

At the weekly luncheon of the Republican Policy Committee on May 2, Percy, Javits and Senator Hugh Scott of Pennsylvania prepared for discussion a nine-point memorandum on Vietnam, which not only took into account the necessity for pressing for an Asian conference and United States efforts to end the war, but also said that "debate of the issues on their merits is essential to a free society." It was the beginning of a gentle but insistent pressure on the Republican Congressional leadership to seek a GOP consensus on the war and to abandon the total bipartisan responsibility that had been Republican policy for several years. Whatever else may have been the merits of such a suggestion to the leadership, it was politically attractive. Bipartisan support of the war had been an attractive idea in 1965 and 1966, when it looked as if the war were going to be over by the time Presidential elections rolled around in 1968. Now it was becoming obvious that instead of the GOP being able to take some of the credit for ending the war in Vietnam, the party would have to shoulder some of the blame for its continuation.

For a long time, Everett Dirksen and House Republican leader Gerald R. Ford of Michigan had backed the President. But the mood of the country was beginning to shift, and they were beginning to shift with it. "That pile of pine boxes is just getting too high in my district" was the way one Congressman who had backed the President put it. In August, Percy told a visitor that the Senate was feeling the sea change, that Mark Hatfield, on a trip back to Oregon a few weeks earlier, had found that the people who had damned him a few months earlier for opposing President Johnson's conduct of the war were saying to him, "You know, you were right all along."

Dirksen was also reported to be feeling the political pressure. Although he denounced suggestions for negotiations and bombing halts and criticisms of the President as "irresponsible," he nonetheless was saying privately that a reassessment of the Republican attitude might be necessary. It would not be until November, however, that he would voice such thoughts publicly, stating in a speech in Grand Rapids, Michigan, that either the United States should push toward a total victory or seek a way to come to the conference table with honor. Such a statement from Dirksen meant that a true shift in thinking was taking place in the high councils of the party. In part, it echoed what Ford had said in August—that the President should either take the wraps off all the targets or seek a way out. Some in Washington felt that this was an indication that the GOP leadership was preparing a dramatic change, since what Ford was telling the President in effect was: "Either you do something we know you aren't going to do or we will start urging you to get out."

Behind the scenes at this time, Percy, Morton and others were moving to try to establish—before the 1968 political campaign was well under way—some form of party unity. It was in this climate that Percy, in a speech on the Senate floor on October 2, listed "seven failures" by the President to win national support for the war. It was, on his part, an attempt not only to express his own views and those of the other moderates in the Senate, but to present a platform for party unity and a draft plan for whatever 1968 might bring:

"Last Friday night President Johnson made a strong argument against unilateral withdrawal from Vietnam. But few Americans and few, if any, in the Congress, are asking for unilateral withdrawal. By suggesting that his critics want unilateral withdrawal, the President is attempting to discredit them all.

"Today more than half the American people disapprove the manner in which the President is conducting the war, but only about 10 percent favor unilateral withdrawal. The President's problem is with the vast majority who are dissatisfied with his performance in Vietnam, not with the 10 percent who urge withdrawal.

"How has the President failed to win the support of the majority for his war in Vietnam? I would say that the President has had seven failures in Vietnam, and these failures are at the root of his problem with the American people:

"*First* is his failure to persuade the South Vietnamese government to institute truly democratic reforms which would win the support of people of their own country.

"*Second* is his failure to persuade the South Vietnamese Army to carry its rightful share of the combat, so that our American men won't have to bear the heaviest burden of the fighting themselves.

"*Third* is his failure to persuade our other Asian allies to participate substantially in the military, economic, psychological and diplomatic tasks confronting us in Vietnam. Further, he has been unable to persuade a single country in Western Europe to provide any meaningful help or support.

"*Fourth* is his failure to pursue every possibility for negotiations leading to a settlement of the war.

"*Fifth* is his failure to learn from experience that every U.S. escalation is matched by the enemy and only brings more casualties.

"*Sixth* is his failure to recognize that bombing so near China has already caused the Chinese and the Soviets to massively increase their military role in support of Hanoi. Thus, for limited military gain, he has provoked heavier pressure against our own forces.

"*Seventh* is his failure to understand that widespread dissent indicates something may be wrong with his policy, rather than with his critics.

"These are the seven failures of Lyndon Johnson in his Vietnam policy. He is not being criticized for refusing to withdraw unilaterally. He is being criticized because he has failed to succeed either with military force or with diplomatic initiative."

In December, 1967, Percy included Vietnam in a seven-nation, round-the-world tour, and came back with some of his views modified. He was still adamant about the necessity for the war to be fought and won by the South Vietnamese, but he had softened his stand on bombing the North.

He said on his return that he believed the best method of testing the peace feelers that were apparently coming out of Hanoi at the New Year would be to halt the bombing of population centers in the North, but to continue hitting the infiltration routes. To propose a total halt to the bombing, he said, would give the North Vietnamese too great a military advantage in supplying their troops and the Vietcong in South Vietnam.

This shift in mood, although not substantive, was perhaps brought on by the persuasion of the military and diplomats in Saigon, or through a realization that a dovelike position in 1968 was not going to be in line with what most of the party believed.

But it may have been brought on by another factor—the fact that he had been shot at. In a village where he had gone by helicopter with a refugee official, an aide, a friend from Chicago, a photographer and Mrs. Percy, the Vietcong threw in several mortar rounds and some small-arms fire as the party—except for Mrs. Percy—walked through the village.

Percy ducked for cover, and the refugee official, Dennis Smith, handed him a revolver. The helicopter took off immediately to take Mrs. Percy to safety, leaving one United States Senator on the ground. The party was flown out, without casualties, a quarter-hour later, but it earned for Percy a major distinction—he became the first leading Republican Presidential possibility to have been under fire in Vietnam.

CHAPTER 15

The Senator—
Politics of the Future

When Percy first took his seat as the ninety-seventh ranking Senator (last was Mark Hatfield, who had stayed home for the inauguration of his successor as Governor of Oregon), he found himself already suffering from a peculiar brand of credibility gap. It was the same problem that Senator Robert Kennedy had: any time there was talk of the Presidency, no one really believed his denials. In Kennedy's case, however, there was historic precedent. It is practically impossible to deny a nomination to an incumbent President if he wants it, and thus the junior Senator from New York could cite chapter and verse, if he wanted to, on exactly why he couldn't push a bid for the nomination in 1968, and make perfect sense while he was doing it.

Percy's was a somewhat different case. It was not in his personality to behave any way but the way he did—like an active, articulate, virile, attractive politician—a model young Senator. This is not to say that Kennedy was not any of these things—quite the contrary. The difference was that the Democratic nomination in 1968 was not up for grabs and the Republican nomination was. So Percy found himself more and more being labeled a "Republican Bobby Kennedy," without the political fortress that American history had built for Kennedy.

On Election Day a Percy campaign aide, with anything but misplaced confidence, composed a memo to his boss on how he should behave when he went to Washington. As quoted by Broder and Hess, it read this way:

> As a Senator-elect, there is one quality you *must* refine to perfection: HUMILITY. No matter what you were or may be, as a newly elected Senator, you are a wretched worm. The Senate absolutely delights in destroying big-shot, small-state governors and red-hot businessmen-politicians. The rules for success are these:
> 1. HUMILITY
> 2. DO YOUR HOMEWORK IN COMMITTEE
> 3. LISTEN, DON'T TALK
> 4. SHOW GREAT DEFERENCE TO YOUR INCUMBENT COLLEAGUES
> 5. DISCLAIM ALL EXPERTISE
> 6. HUMILITY

Two weeks later, however, Percy burst upon the Washington scene like Halley's comet. He held a press conference, and the headlines and stories treated him like something entirely new. Later, the freshman tried to offset some of this wild talk of "a Presidential dark horse," and "Percy disavows Presidential ambition, but—." Figuratively rubbing his great toe in the dust, he said he was "just a fellow trying to be a good Senator," a standard remark he had used even since before his election.

Every columnist and political reporter in Washington had a crack at the Illinois freshman in the opening weeks of the Ninetieth Congress, and generally they liked what they saw. Typical was a lengthy piece in the *Wall Street Journal* in March, which quoted the Republican chairman of a Western state as "lackadaisically" reciting the strengths and weaknesses of the GOP front-runners. Then, with his eyes shining, the chairman said: "You know the man I really like? That young fellow, Percy."

The author of the article, Alan L. Otten, called Percy "a fascinating phenomenon," and said that when it came to Presidential availability, Percy was doing very little to discourage interest. Speeches, interviews and television appearances "all seem calculated to encourage it. What these display is an attractive product. He's young and good-looking, with the scrubbed appeal of a Jack Armstrong, All-American Boy. He's intelligent and energetic, comes across particularly well on television with a deep, clear voice and polished manner." Although Otten went on to say that the Percy assets were largely the result of liabilities in other GOP candidates and that this shining Percy image could tarnish quickly, the space (nearly two columns on the *Journal's* editorial page) and the attention given to Percy far outstripped that given any other freshman since Bob and Ted Kennedy arrived in Washington.

And when it came to the Presidency, Percy, while denying any interest, was, by his actions, discouraging any lessening of speculation. Those who wrote wanting to form Percy-for-President organizations were sent letters which said: "As much as I appreciate your kind intentions, I sincerely and earnestly urge you not open a 'Percy for President' headquarters. I am not a candidate for the nomination, I have no intention of becoming a candidate and I strongly feel that an office of this type would be both inappropriate and misleading."

Nevertheless, the Percy out-of-state speaking schedule grew— New Hampshire, Michigan, Nebraska, Kentucky, California, Illinois, New York, New Jersey, Pennsylvania and points east, west, north and south. There was even a trip to England in January.

These speeches were generally in behalf of the Republican party and carried such titles as "The Future of the Republican Party," "A Call for Unity" and the like. To offset any speculation that this was, Heaven forfend, a campaign by Percy for national exposure, his office dropped, early in the game, the practice of issuing texts from Washington; GOP leaders who were close supporters of Percy were carefully avoiding any mention of the Presidency by referring to him in such terms as "the top salesman the party has these days"—and the label would seem to have been accurate, since his appearance at a fund-raising dinner was generally guaranteed to sell tickets.

Nor were the speeches particularly fiery and important, as far as strong statements of issues were concerned; the audiences were generally too partisan or too split for that. A reporter, asking Percy's Washington office if the text of one such out-of-town speech was going to be available, was told by a Percy aide that it was not and that the speech would not provide any headlines. The aide's appraisal was correct. It was a standard, let's-all-be-good-Republicans-together effort.

Nevertheless, the speaking schedule was a departure from a post-election promise by Percy that he would not be making speeches around the country. He had felt, when he was elected, that he had been asked by the party to run and that he really didn't owe the GOP anything. In addition, there was, in December, 1966, a gnawing and understandable worry about personal security. He did not plan to spend a night away from his family, he said. Later, when the question of the earlier promise was raised, while Percy was making extensive tours, the change was explained on the basis of security, that Percy now felt he and his family were sufficiently safe to permit some travel.

"What the moderate leaders of the party are trying to do with Chuck," said a senior GOP Senate staff member in the spring of 1967, "is to bring him along as the spokesman for our wing on such things as urban problems and foreign affairs—housing, Vietnam, East-West trade, tariffs. But they also plan to guard him pretty carefully until he learns how to protect himself in the clinches in Washington, and learning that can be a painful process. No, if people like Morton and Case and Senators like them can take the flak while Percy is making their positions known, it will be the best way to develop him as a Senator. Besides, they're getting to be pretty tired voices, some of them, and he's a fresh face in Washington and in the country."

Beyond that, intended or not, Percy's national reputation was beginning to climb, not so much as a 1968 Presidential candidate, but as good, solid Presidential timber, possibly a good bet for Vice President on someone else's ticket. As Otten and other writers had pointed out, this was largely due to the shifts and changes that were going on inside the ranks of the front-runners for the 1968 nomination.

Romney, who had appeared in 1966 to be the best bet for the moderates, was beginning to falter in the stretch. He was, in the words of one Washington correspondent, "doing too much of his thinking in public," making statements that left him increasingly naked, politically speaking. These statements culminated in the fall of 1967 with a remark that he had been "brainwashed" by administration diplomatic and military leaders on Vietnam two years before and that the "brainwashing" had stayed with him. His Presidential backers—Rockefeller, Javits, Scott—were horrified, and sent him off on a tour of the nation's ghettos, with a warning not to talk too much, so he listened hard (his "Lemmy-ask-ya-this" was making reporters covering the tour cringe after the first week) and came out ready to make a formal announcement. The hope was, of course, to keep the Michigan Governor strong enough through a few primaries so that even if the showing he made was not the strongest one imaginable, it could at least be used by the moderates to make a preconvention or convention deal with the conservatives on a candidate who might be suitable to both parties, very possibly Chuck Percy.

But the voters of California, on Election Day, 1966, changed that thinking, without anyone's realizing it until quite a time later. Ronald Reagan, the former actor, had rolled up a margin of 993,739 votes to knock out the re-election bid by Governor Edmund G. (Pat) Brown. Reagan was a conservative of the first water, and he was as good-looking as Percy and a familiar, white-hatted figure on the Late Show, with a smile whose earlier public beneficiaries, long before he got to the Governor's chair in Sacramento, included Ann Sheridan, Shirley Temple and Bonzo, the chimpanzee.

By mid-1967 Reagan had ceased to be a cloud no bigger than Barry Goldwater's hand on the national political horizon and was a serious contender, although he publicly denied it. There was talk of a write-in candidacy for him in New Hampshire, of primary appearances in other states. There was a nationwide speaking tour, and a cruise aboard the S. S. *Independence*, along with all but a few other U.S. governors, showed him to have the same Wheaties-eating image that Percy had. Besides, his increasing popularity gave heart to the conservatives that here they might have a Goldwater who could win.

Thus a strong showing by Nixon and Reagan in primaries could leave the moderates—and particularly the Eastern Establishment— with no honors in their hand with which to make a bid; the pre-convention picture could easily be a face-off between two relative conservatives unless the governors, generally sold on the moderate cause, could speak with an authoritative voice at the convention.

For nearly a decade the conservative Westerners in the GOP had been trying to wrest the kingmaking powers from the Eastern Establishment—that collection of politicians, businessmen, philanthropists and academicians who had traditionally named the Presidential nominee. When Rockefeller, by reason of name and record a charter member of the Establishment, had gone shopping for support before the 1960 convention, he found that the Middle West and Far West were already locked up for Nixon. Therefore he had to use what powers remained to him and to the Establishment to put across the strongest kind of moderate platform. In 1964 it was apparent the control was gone; the Establishment could make no more than an impotent, if frenzied and courageous, show of force against the Goldwaterites. By 1966, with the election of Reagan, the basic control of the GOP had crossed the Great Divide and had moved into California, or, more specifically, Southern California. This was a great conservative breadbasket of votes.

But it was much more than that. Draw a circle a hundred miles in radius around the City of Our Lady of the Angels. Within it lie half the population of the state of California, a booming economy and more money in personal income than any one state but five— New York, Illinois, Michigan, Pennsylvania and, of course, the whole of California. This meant power for the conservatives, power to open headquarters, to buy television time, to organize and staff a hundred "Citizens Committees" and "Volunteers for . . ." It was no wonder that the moderates were beginning to quail at the sight of Reagan drawing the big crowds, the loud cheers, the steady increase in popularity in the polls.

Percy's position in this shift was less than ideal, although not hopeless. For three years he had associated himself with the Establishment, not only because it represented his basic political thinking, particularly in its internationalist bent, but because it was a club to which any poor boy who had worked his way up through the business and political ranks would like to belong.

He had lunched with members of the editorial board of the *New York Times* and with top editors of *Time* and *Newsweek*. Their cachet was, to him, invaluable, and during the campaign of 1966, when the *Times*, in a rare move, wrote an editorial endorsing Douglas, Percy tried to carry it off with a smile, but the hurt was obvious. On the downstate campaign special train, he referred at whistle stop after whistle stop to the endorsement, saying what a fine paper the *Times* was, but always adding that he would rather have the endorsement of the paper in whatever town he happened to be in than that of the *New York Times*. ("Methinks the candidate doth protest too much," said one reporter, hearing the peroration for the fifteenth or sixteenth time.)

Later, in the Senate, his positions were often similar to those of leading members of the Establishment. He warred with Dirksen openly on high tariffs, but it was a position he had taken consistently for two decades. His position on Vietnam might eventually get him into trouble with the Eisenhower wing of the party, since it meant repudiating the foreign policy of the only successful GOP President in nearly half a century, but it was a position which took him away from Reagan and Dirksen and Goldwater and put him closer to the intellectuals of the Establishment.

In April, 1967, Percy organized a conference of top New York businessmen to gain support for his housing program. The list of conferees included such names as David Rockefeller, Keith Funston and others who were long-time, ranking members of the Establishment. At the same time, he received a personally conducted tour of some of Manhattan's worst ghettos from Mayor Lindsay. Lindsay had long had a high regard for Percy, personally and as a fellow urbanist, but the helicopter and walking tour was a high political compliment. (Later, when Romney made a similar tour, Lindsay took no official recognition of the visit, except to send an assistant press secretary to help the Michigan Governor with the rampaging New York radio and TV reporters.) Percy, both as a candidate and as a Senator, was generally careful to ignore, at least as far as reporters were concerned, any interpretive stories that he did not like. But after the New York trip he called one reporter personally after the reporter had suggested that the conference might have political overtones. The retort was that by that time in Percy's career almost anything he did had political overtones.

"The best way for a fallback candidate to get himself nominated," said one of the wisest Senate Republican staffers in 1967, "is to be sure he is not identified early as a fallback candidate." Politically, this was a major problem for Percy. Rockefeller was seemingly totally unacceptable to the conservatives, Scranton was out of the running and there was practically no one left. So the spotlight, fairly or unfairly, was on Percy throughout 1967, and whatever he did was being weighed and measured for its present or future political value.

Curiously enough, Percy had, by speaking without thinking of the full consequence of his words, caused his relationship with Rockefeller to slip rather badly. The New York Governor had never really been warm toward Percy, but in 1967, on several occasions in New York, the new Senator had tried to heal the long-standing coolness by referring in speeches to Rockefeller as the "best-qualified man in the party to be President." There is no evidence to suppose that Percy was doing anything but trying to be complimentary and that he believed what he said, but Rockefeller took it as an attempt to undercut his support of Romney and was visibly annoyed. Nor did Lindsay help matters greatly at a background session with reporters in Washington in the fall of 1967, when he said that someone with more or less dovish views on Vietnam, like Percy, ought to be the 1968 nominee. However, aside from his affection for Percy, Lindsay liked on occasion to remind Rockefeller that there was another major Republican in the Empire State.

Reporters in Washington and elsewhere soon tired of asking the freshman Senator what his plans were for the Presidency; they knew the answers they would get. But by assiduous questioning of staff aides and putting two and two together, it could fairly be assumed that during his first year as a Senator, Percy's private attitude was one of listening a great deal and trying to say nothing that would upset the apple cart, one way or another. He denied, probably honestly, that he was an active candidate, but he certainly kept all the options open.

And common sense would seem to dictate that even this must have been a difficult task. From one, two or three removes, it is easy to talk about someone's qualifications to occupy the most awesome office in the world. But when one is actually in the position of being the person talked about, the mere suggestion by serious and responsible people that one is qualified to be the President of the United States must be the most heady wine imaginable. To stay cool, to watch and listen and not bolt, like some Midwestern George A. Wallace, into an ill-conceived and ill-timed stampeding race, must have required the most enormous self-discipline. And that kind of self-discipline Percy, a relative neophyte in national politics and an effervescent person in his own right, obviously possessed in significant amounts in those first exciting months in Washington.

There were miscues in the first year as Senator, but none of them major ones. On "Meet the Press," for example, a few days after he took his seat, Percy gave a lame answer on the desirability of halting the bombing of North Vietnam. He was one of five Republican freshman Senators on the panel; two (Edward Brooke and Mark Hatfield) said it should be halted, while Howard Baker and Clifford Hansen said it should be continued. Percy said the attacks hadn't done any good, but they probably should be continued, an answer which led Capitol Hill wags to say that the five GOP freshmen had "split two-and-a-half to two-and-a-half" in their answers. Early in the session, too, he found himself voting with the Republican conservatives and the Southern Democrats on the issue of suspension of filibustering on civil-rights legislation, a vote which, although it was probably due more to inexperience in Senate infighting than anything else, was nonetheless criticized by his moderate colleagues in the party.

In Illinois, and particularly among the Congressional Republican delegation, there was criticism of Percy's staff—that telephone calls were not being returned, that there was no liaison, that Percy was so interested in his housing bills and Vietnam proposals that he was ignoring the home folks. But again, common sense would dictate that it takes years to build a good Senate staff, a smooth-running organization which is simultaneously wise in the ways of Capitol Hill, national politics and the needs of constituents. On Percy's staff there were ideological splits and difficulties in shaking down. There was worry, too, about the amount of money that was being invested out of Percy's own pocket; the estimated figure was $75,000 the first year. But a Senator from a large state like Illinois needs more than the meager government allowance, especially a freshman who does not have a call on a large committee staff whose efforts can be diverted to his own use.

Houser, the veteran campaign manager, stayed on in a key spot as Percy's eyes and ears in Illinois, a post of both political and legislative sensitivity in state and national affairs. In Washington, Percy had Allen J. Marrinson, thirty-four, who had dabbled in GOP politics in Chicago, as administrative assistant and office manager. He, like Houser, was a graduate of Northwestern Law School, had served as an Assistant U.S. Attorney in Chicago and been vice president of a Chicago bank. Scott Cohen, forty-three, was the principal adviser on foreign policy, a post for which he had trained as a newspaperman and during fourteen years with the Central Intelligence Agency, both in overt and covert operations. As legislative assistant, particularly on domestic affairs, Percy chose Martin

R. Hoffman, also thirty-four, who had been chief minority counsel to the House Committee on the Judiciary. Hoffman was hired on the recommendation of Percy's close political associate on the North Shore, Representative Donald Rumsfeld. Also handling legislation was Carol Khosrovi, who had worked in a number of Congressional staff posts, including the office of Representative Robert A. Taft, Jr. Cal Fentress, twenty-nine, a former *Newsweek* editor and writer and a long-standing friend and associate, stayed on from the campaign staff as principal speech writer and press aide. In addition, Percy had the services of Duff Reed, thirty-seven, who had been assigned by his boss, Senator Morton, to help out all five GOP freshmen with press relations, but as time went on Percy was occupying most of Reed's time. And, of course, on the housing bill there was McClaughry.

Almost as Chicago had never been, Washington was becoming a natural element for Percy and his family. There was the pleasant brick house in Georgetown, although the specter of security was still very much with the family; no mention made of schools the younger children were attending, no mention of the watchdog's name for fear someone might entice it away by calling it. There were dinner parties for which a young, attractive Senator and his equally attractive and younger wife were very much in demand, parties at which the good conversation bubbles and flows, a chance to relax a bit after nearly four years of political effort to climb the political ladder to this high rung. When Percy told a visitor that he was "having more darned fun" with his housing bill, the remark could equally be applied to the rest of his life in Washington. He had become a United States Senator, and there are only ninety-nine others like him in the world.

There were family pleasures, too. Sharon, Valerie's twin, a sparkling, outgoing blonde with the best sense of humor in the family, in April married Jay Rockefeller, a serious and charming young man who was engaged in the War on Poverty and was a member of the West Virginia House of Delegates. Percy was extremely close to his new son-in-law, and there was a genuine mutual admiration society in the relationship. Rockefeller had consulted Percy on his decision to go into politics from the poverty program, and Percy had delighted in spending long evenings talking with him about it. (Percy even had a little fun at his son-in-law's expense in speeches about the relationship. "Some of my best friends are Democrats," he told audiences in a jocund manner, "but I didn't expect my daughter to marry one.") In the library of the Percys' Georgetown house were pictures of Sharon and Jay taken during their engagement, on a family vacation at Caneel Bay in the British Virgin Islands. "I guess it shows," wrote Rockefeller on one of the pictures of Sharon and him. It did.

The wedding, at the University of Chicago's Rockefeller Chapel, was a magnificent affair, Chicago's "wedding of the year." In the chapel there was stately music and the solemn, literate vows from the Book of Common Prayer. At the reception, in Ida Noyes Hall, adjacent to the chapel, there was the kind of crush which every bride wants at her wedding, her own friends and her family's friends and the groom's friends standing in line almost to the point of discomfort, but still there. There was also a seemingly unending flow of good champagne and good music to dance to and a jolly, happy ambiance.

But, like the Kennedy family, whatever the Percy family did was too often dogged by tragedy. The day before the wedding, at the Art Institute in Chicago, there had been a ceremony in Valerie's memory. Loraine Percy's mother had been stricken with a heart attack and had died, so that Loraine and her brothers, John and David, attended the service, but not the reception. For the guests, it was a sad development to which lip service was paid; for the family, it was, aside from the loss of one of its major members, a tragic reminder of Valerie and shot a bitter arrow into what should have been an occasion of joy.

One day in February, in the corridor of the Old Senate Office Building, Percy greeted an Illinois reporter who asked the Senator how his Lincoln Day weekend trip to Illinois had gone. It had been Percy's first trip back to his home state since he had taken his seat.

Percy's face lighted up and he replied: "I had a wonderful time! You know, for the first time in three years I wasn't asking people for something. I was asking them what I could do for *them*. It's a great feeling!"

This relaxation, this acclimatization to Washington and the new life in the Senate, was a hallmark of Percy's career in his first year in Washington. During the long, three-year fight to win elective office, he had been, for the most part, tense and serious, as if everything in the world were riding on his success, which, indeed, it was for him. When he was campaigning, his sense of humor tended, like many other politicians', to center around jokes that he told himself, and he never seemed quite sure whether or not he should laugh at something that someone else had said. At home, however, he was different during those years. Close friends have described his humor as being of the "somewhat zany, giggly variety—very real and not particularly what you might expect from a man who is so exalted in business and in the world generally." This was his private humor, and as Percy became more used to his job, it tended to become his public humor as well—perhaps not zany and giggly, but at least it was more relaxed, more attuned to give and take than merely to telling a few snappy gags that someone else had provided. (In one case, however, he got badly caught. In a speech in Nebraska that was widely reported in Washington, it was made embarrassingly clear in newspaper stories that he had lifted, verbatim and without credit, a series of jokes which Robert Kennedy had told on himself a few nights earlier. But after some initial embarrassment, he made a joke out of his theft.)

For a freshman Senator, he was moving fast and high in his party's upper echelons. He did his homework well and was an avid, informed persuader. On most issues—housing, Vietnam, urban problems, tariffs, foreign policy in general—he stated his positions clearly and stuck with them, despite the Olympian thunder of such people as Everett McKinley Dirksen. Early in the year, veteran political strategist F. Clifton White gave Percy a piece of second-hand advice. "If I were Chuck Percy," he said, "I'd watch Dirksen's water glass every day. As soon as the level went down a quarter of an inch, I'd be there filling it up."

But to Percy, Dirksen represented a stripe of political thinking with which he did not care to be associated. Although the two Senators opened a joint downstate office in Centralia, it was never, despite some mutual praise on public occasions, an easy relationship. There were too many things dividing them, and Dirksen was convinced that Percy was actively running for President from the time he arrived in Washington. Indeed, in the Gridiron Club show in March, the reporter playing Dirksen sang plaintively, to the tune of "My Bonnie Lies Over the Ocean":

Chuck Percy is only a freshman.
As junior as junior can be.
So why does he act like the leader?
Oh, bring back Paul Douglas to me.

It would have been easy for Percy to fill Dirksen's water glass and not to act the leader. But for whatever reasons, he chose not to. Perhaps the Senate staff aide who said Percy would be remiss if he waited until Senate tradition caught up with him was right. The seniority system has deep roots and is not easily moved. But it can be moved. Paul Douglas had shown how.

With persistence and as much diplomacy as he felt the situation warranted, Percy had pushed his housing bill as fast and as far as he could. He had earned the reputation of a hustler, and yet of a man who could be prevailed upon without a great deal of argument to take a break in the early morning or evening for tennis with fellow Senators. On Vietnam, he was speaking strongly, with none of the equivocation that had characterized some of his campaign statements on other matters. He was finding his feet fast.

Percy also won some plaudits for his voting record in his first year, siding with liberal Democrats and Republicans and generally against Dirksen on such key issues as lobbying control, the U.S.-Soviet consular treaty, the treaty on peaceful uses of outer space and amendments to substitute a voluntary system for the draft. He had one black mark against him, however, on cloture, and another one on a reapportionment amendment sponsored by Senator Edward M. Kennedy of Massachusetts liberalizing election laws. On the latter, he voted with Dirksen.

But the free-swinging liberal publication *Focus/Midwest*, published in St. Louis, praised his liberal record. "The most engrossing development has been Percy's voting behavior," the magazine said. "He follows a policy obviously independent of Illinois' senior senator. Except for the one vote cited [on the Kennedy amendment], his record—in Congress at least—could not have been bested by former Senator Paul Douglas."

Nationally, too, Percy was beginning to widen his base, to become known. His speeches, while not often covered by the national press, were finding significant space in newspapers and radio and television broadcasts whenever he made them. And all the time, those who wanted him to make a bid for higher office were keeping up a gentle but insistent pressure. His attitude of watching and waiting was coupled with a vague plan, that was only beginning to form in mid-1967, based on seeing what the future brought, what happened to other Republicans in the running for the Presidency. If Romney stubbed his toe in the New Hampshire and Wisconsin primaries in the spring of 1968, Percy would sound out Rockefeller and then make up his mind what he would do. It all had to be played with tact and delicacy, for Percy was still too far down on the list of candidates to be able to make an overt move early in the 1968 race. But sometime he would have to make that decision.

There is a basic rule of politics that the would-be candidate cannot always pick his time to move or let others pick it for him. Fate has a way of taking a hand; a Corsican second lieutenant of artillery finds himself an emperor; a hen-pecked prairie lawyer makes some speeches on slavery and finds himself the President chosen to hold the Union together; a blunt Missouri Senator, hard-working but uninspiring, is made President through the death of the strongest Chief Magistrate the Republic ever had and becomes a leader of the free world.

Predictions in politics are idle. Arthur Schlesinger, Jr., talking of the difficulty of guessing what might take place in 1972 in Presidential politics, said to an interviewer in 1967: "Suppose we were having this conversation in 1940, and trying to guess who would be the next three Presidents after Franklin Roosevelt. To be right, we would have to have picked a Senator fighting for his life in a Democratic primary in Missouri, an obscure staff-grade officer of the United States Army and a kid still in college."

The political winds blow across the land, sometimes here and sometimes there, and often the figures that have looked so promising at one time become like tumbleweed, pushed hither and yon without respite or direction. But others who look promising fight the winds or, like sailors, use them to set their own course and speed.

What Percy's role may be in the next few years no one can possibly predict with any degree of certainty. But he has never been a man who has let others set his course and speed.

Index

CHARLES PERCY OF ILLINOIS

by David Murray

Senator Charles Percy's life puts storybooks to shame. When he was twelve, his family became one of the dole-supported "new poor" of the Depression. He used a variety of entrepreneurial ventures to pay his way through the University of Chicago. The president of Bell & Howell, Percy's teacher in a Christian Science Sunday school, had been so impressed by the boy that he gave him a summer job answering complaint letters. Percy was president of the company before he was thirty, on his way to a position of considerable influence in national business and political affairs. In 1960 Percy played an important role in drafting the Republican platform (with General Eisenhower as his mentor) and, after an unsuccessful bid for the governorship